Ruddy Somali kitten

AN ILLUSTRATED GUIDE TO

CATS

Seal Tabby-point Colourpoint (Siamese) Shorthair

Blue-eyed White Persian (Longhair)

AN ILLUSTRATED GUIDE TO
CATS

**A practical guide designed to help you select
and care for the most suitable cat for you and your home
Featuring over 100 breeds and colors**

Dorothy Silkstone Richards

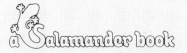

a Salamander book

Published by Arco Publishing, Inc.
NEW YORK

A Salamander Book

Published by
Arco Publishing, Inc.,
219 Park Avenue South,
New York,
N.Y. 10003,
United States of America.

©1982 by Salamander Books Ltd.,
27 Old Gloucester Street,
London WC1N 3AF,
United Kingdom.

This book may not be sold outside
the USA and Canada.

All rights reserved.

Library of Congress catalog card
number 81 71940

ISBN 0 668 05418 2

All correspondence concerning
the content of this volume should
be addressed to Salamander
Books Ltd.

Publisher's note: This book is
based upon the material appearing
in *A Cat of Your Own*.

Credits

Author: Dorothy Silkstone
Richards B.Sc. writes about cats
from practical experience, for until
recently Mrs. Richards bred
Burmese at her home in Bedford,
England. Dorothy has written two
books on cat breeding and co-
authored one on Burmese cats.
Many years serving on the
committees of various cat clubs
and the Pet Trade Association, first
hand experience of boarding all
breeds and wide ranging travels
have given Dorothy a valuable
insight into the problems and
temperaments of all breeds of cats.

Consultant: Charleane Beane has
a wide knowledge of the American
cat scene and is a regular
contributor to the authoritative
International Cat Fancy Magazine.

Editor: Geoff Rogers
Designer: Roger Hyde

Color artwork and line drawings:
John Francis (Linden Artists).
©Salamander Books Ltd.

Photographs: Most of the photographs have been taken by Marc
Henrie. A full list of credits appears
on page 160.

**Color and monochrome
reproductions:** Rodney Howe Ltd.,
England.

Filmset: Modern Text Typesetting
Ltd., Essex, England.

Printed in Belgium by
Henri Proost & Cie, Turnhout.

Contents

Text and color artwork illustrations are cross-referenced throughout as follows: 64▸ Page numbers in Roman type refer to text entries; those in **bold** type to color artwork illustrations.

Introduction

This guide to cats is intended to help you to choose the right cat for you, your family and your life-style. Unlike dogs, cats are all of a similar size, and cost approximately the same to feed. But some longhairs take a long time to groom; other cats need more freedom; and a few are extremely vocal. The good points are listed under each breed, and a 'take heed' section warns you of any possible disadvantages.

Temperament
All cats are intelligent, lovable and companionable. Some are shy, sweet and docile; others are demanding, vocal, active and sometimes exasperating. Read the section on temperament to make sure you choose a cat that the whole family will enjoy.

Body types
There are two extreme body types. One is cobby, low on the leg, broad-shouldered, round-headed, personified by the Persian and the Exotic shorthair. The other is the svelte, lithe, muscular, small-boned, narrow-headed cat, such as the Siamese and Balinese. All other cats are between these two extremes.

Deformities
Some natural mutations have occurred, which are really deformities but have been perpetuated for long enough to become acceptable (eg, the tailless Manx) or were considered sufficiently attractive to perpetuate from choice (eg, the Scottish Fold and the Japanese Bobtail in the USA).

Coat types
There are five basic coat types:
Longhair, between 5 and 15cm (2-6in) long, which must have daily grooming. This type has been around for centuries.
Shorthair, which is much easier to groom, but benefits from lots of hand stroking. This is the oldest known coat type.
Curly, as in the Devon Rex and the Cornish Rex. (There is also a Si-Rex, which is a Siamese with a curly coat.) Such coats have been known since the 1950s.
Wirehaired cats were the result of a natural mutation that appeared in 1966.
Hairless cats are thought attractive in Canada, but are hard to get elsewhere. They have been bred since the 1960s.

Coat pattern
Having decided which body and coat type you prefer, you must now choose the coat pattern. The possibilities are:
Self or solid coloured, which is the same colour from the tips to the roots of the hairs, all over.
Tipped, where the fur nearest the skin is one colour and the ends are another colour. Lightly tipped cats are known as Chinchillas, medium tipped ones are Shadeds, and very heavily tipped ones are Smokes.
Tabby includes four different patterns: Classic tabby has clearly defined markings as on page 81; Mackerel tabby has vertical

stripes down the sides; Spotted tabby has broken stripes becoming spots; and Ticked tabby has several bands of colour on each hair.

Van or Piebald pattern is almost white with patches of colour(s).
Bicolour is white with one other colour, in defined proportions.
Particoloured cats are of more than one colour.
Himalayan is a well-known coat pattern; the face (mask), ears, legs and tail are in a contrasting colour to the rest of the body.
Himalayan-and-white resulted when the white spotting gene was introduced to the Himalayan, and results in white feet.
Combination coat is any usual coat pattern with white.
Torbie or Patched tabby is Tabby with Tortoiseshell.

Colour

Using today's knowledge of genetics, we can combine almost any body type with any coat type and any pattern in any colour. The basic colours are white, black, blue, red, cream, chocolate, lilac, brown and varying shades of brown. Eye colour usually goes with coat colour, but breeders can now produce a different eye colour almost to order.

Nomenclature and classification

The same cats are known by different names in various parts of the world, so we have used the American name first, followed by the others. Longhair cobby cats are known as 'Persian' in the USA and as 'Longhair' in the UK, and we have called them Persian (Longhair) for the breeds that have been established a long time. New breeds have sometimes been given a new name, although they may have the same standard as the Persian, such as the Colourpoint. Self-coloured Persians (Longhairs) are grouped together except the Self-Chocolate and Self-Lilac, which are called Kashmir in the USA, purely because they appeared during the Colourpoint breeding programme. Other colours that appeared at this time were the Chocolate Tortie and the Lilac-cream (strictly speaking, a Lilac Tortie). All are Persian or Longhair in type, and future generations may well wonder why in some countries these were separated.

Shorthair cats with Himalayan coat pattern are known throughout the world as Siamese, except in the USA, where the Seal, Blue, Chocolate and Lilac points are Siamese but any other point colour is called Colourpoint Shorthair; similarly, in the USA only the Seal, Blue, Chocolate and Lilac longhair Siamese are called Balinese, and other point colours are Javanese. In the UK, self-coloured Orientals are 'Foreign', but all the others are called Oriental Shorthairs, regardless of coat pattern or colour; in the USA, all these are Oriental Shorthairs. Also, all the new colours of the Burmese are known as Malayans in the USA.

There is also a confusion about the names of the colours: what are known as Champagne, Platinum/Lavender and Sable in the USA are known as the genetic colours Chocolate, Lilac and Brown in the UK.

PERSIAN (Longhair)

Good points
- *Beautiful and elegant*
- *Affectionate*
- *Undemanding*
- *Suitable for apartment life*

Take heed
- *Needs daily grooming*
- *Vulnerable*
- *Moults*
- *Does not like to be teased*

The Persian makes an attractive, sweet and undemanding pet. It is docile, quiet, companionable and elegant. It likes being with people and is generally good tempered, unless teased. However, it must be protected from dogs and traffic because, with its short legs and rather heavy body, it cannot always escape quickly.

However, the Persian is quieter and less adventurous than some of its shorthaired cousins, and can often be kept in a fenced area of the garden from which a longer legged cat would escape, though the cat should not be permanently penned up on its own. A Persian will also live happily in an apartment, provided it is given the run of the place and plenty of fresh air.

The Persian's main disadvantage for a busy person is that it *must* be groomed daily. The cat will moult all year, but especially in the summer months, and if it swallows large quantities of hair, fur balls may form and cause an obstruction in the stomach that, in extreme cases, would have to be removed surgically. When it runs free outside, because of its short legs leaves and debris may be caught up in the long fur, and if left, will knot up into hard balls. Their removal will then be very painful for the cat.

Consequently, owning a Persian is quite a responsibility, but if you have plenty of time to look after one, then you will be sure to find it

Left: A Cream-and-white Bicolour Persian with a magnificent coat. This is one of the newer colours.

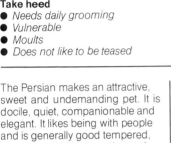

an excellent, loving and devoted companion.

Persians are not as prolific as some of the shorthaired or foreign varieties, and therefore may cost more to buy. However, if you want a pet rather than a show champion, it is possible to purchase a non-show class kitten, which will make a super pet, much more cheaply.

Grooming
Daily grooming is essential and involves removing any knots and tangles (which may not always be readily visible) with a wide-toothed comb, then using a fine-toothed comb to remove dead hairs and finally giving the coat a good brush with a long-handled pure bristle brush (as this gives rise to less static electricity than brushes with synthetic fibres). The tufts between the toes should be combed carefully, as mats here would be very uncomfortable for the cat. The eyes should be checked regularly, as Persians are prone to blocked tear ducts and any discharge from the eyes will discolour the fur around the nose.

If destined for show, the paler-coloured Persians will benefit from a bath a week before the show, followed by a powdering with fuller's earth or a proprietary non-toxic grooming powder to remove grease marks from the coat. The powder should be rubbed in well down to the roots, then brushed out thoroughly. Pre-show preparation for the darker colours involves the application of bay rum to the coat—not powder, as this may mar the colour. The hair is whipped up with the brush so that every hair stands up away from the body, and frames the face in a most appealing way.

Origin and history

Longhaired cats have been known in Europe since the sixteenth century, but their precise origin remains obscure. Records show that there were two types of long-haired cat, one from Turkey — the Angora — and the other from Persia (now Iran), although it is likely that both these types originated in Russia and were brought by traders to Europe via Asia Minor. Whereas cats with long hair are found today in both Turkey and Iran, they are still much more common in parts of Russia, and it is possible that the harsh climate there may have favoured the evolution of the long coat.

The so-called Persian cats had broader, rounder heads, smaller ears, shorter bodies and plushier coats than the Angoras, and were undoubtedly the forerunners of the modern Persian type. Selective breeding of these cats over the years, particularly in the last 100 years, has produced the typical Persian type and the numerous colour varieties known today. The Persian is one of the oldest and most popular show breeds, and many fine cats bred in the United Kingdom have been exported to form the foundations of breeding lines in Europe, the United States, Australia and New Zealand.

SHOW SUMMARY

General appearance. The show Persian is a sturdy cat of gently curving lines. It is a medium to large cat with a long, flowing coat, an ethereal look and a pretty face.

Coat. Long and thick (up to 15cm/6in in length), but fine, soft and silky, standing away from the body, ideally with every hair separate. The coat should shine with glowing good health. There is a very full ruff forming a halo around the head, and a long frill between the front legs.

Body. Cobby, solid and rounded, low lying on the legs. Deep in the chest; massive across the shoulders and rump. Legs short, thick and strong with straight fore-legs. Feet large, firm, rounded and well tufted.

Tail. Short and full, especially at the base. No kinks.

Head. Broad, round and massive on a short, thick neck. Face round and pretty, with no hint of wedgi-ness. Jaw broad. Chin strong, not undershot. Cheeks full. Nose almost snub, short and broad with a good break or stop where it meets the forehead. The stop is particularly pronounced in American Persians. Ears tiny, rounded at the tips, set wide apart and tilted forward, set low on the head, with long ear tufts.

Eyes. Large, round and set wide apart. Full, brilliant and wide-awake, with a sweet expression. Slanted, oval or deep-set eyes are faults. Eye colour may fade with age.

PERSIAN COLOURS

There are at least 30 colour varieties of Persian at present, although not all are recognized for competition in all countries. In the United Kingdom, each colour variety is re-garded as a separate breed, and classified by the name 'Longhair' rather than Persian, whereas in the United States, colours are listed simply as varieties of Persian.

WHITE PERSIAN

White Persians are very beautiful cats and one of the oldest varieties. They were often regarded as status symbols in London drawing rooms at the turn of the century. White Persians have been known in Europe for about 300 years, but the earliest Whites had blue eyes and long, pointed faces, and were frequently deaf. White cats began to attract attention in the late 1800s and were first shown in London in 1903, at which time they were also becoming popular in the United States.

Today there are three varieties—
Blue-eyed White, Orange-eyed
White and Odd-eyed White (one of
each colour)—due to outcrossing
to other Persians, notably blues. It
seems difficult to breed the good
Persian type with blue eyes, and the
Blue-eyed Whites on the show
bench still have slightly longer ears
and faces, although they usually
have better coats than Orange-eyed
Whites.

One disadvantage of white cats
is that many of the Blue-eyed Whites
are deaf from birth and some of
the odd-eyed cats are deaf on the
blue-eyed side. Deafness may be
difficult to detect at first, because
the cat's other senses may com-
pensate. It is quite a responsibility
to own a deaf cat, because it must
be protected from traffic and other
dangers. It is best to confine such
a cat to your property to avoid any
unforeseen accidents.

Grooming
To keep the cat's coat really white,
dust with talcum powder or a proprietary chalk-based grooming
powder daily, then brush and
comb out thoroughly. Any grease
in the coat of a White Persian will
show up as yellowish marks, particularly on the tail, and especially
in male cats. To remove these

*Above: A splendid Blue-eyed
White Persian well prepared for
showing. Note the magnificent
long frill that encircles the head
and the front of the chest.*

stains, the tail should be washed
in warm water to which a little borax
has been added, and rinsed
thoroughly afterwards.

For a show cat, a bath a few days
before a show will probably be
essential to set the coat off to its
full advantage. Sunlight is unlikely
to spoil the coat, so there is no need
to keep the cat indoors.

Breeding
Blue-eyed Whites have smaller
litters, which may account for the
fact that they are not as numerous
as the Orange-eyed Whites. Their
deafness may also account for
their lack of popularity and unfortunately two cats with normal
hearing may produce deaf kittens.
Unless you are experienced, it is
advisable not to use a deaf cat for
breeding. A deaf queen requires
more supervision than a normal
cat because she cannot hear the
cries of her kittens. She should be
placed on a hard surface covered
with newspaper, so that she can
feel her kittens and the vibrations
of their cries.

Kittens

All the kittens are born with blue eyes and it may be some weeks before you can tell whether there are blue-eyed, orange-eyed or odd-eyed kittens in the litter. The depth of the eye colour also takes some months to develop. Orange eyes should be deep orange or copper, and if a kitten does not have the deep eye colour by the time it is six or seven months old, then it is unlikely that it will intensify later in life. When born the kittens are pinkish in colour, but this baby coat soon disappears and they become covered in lovely fluffy white fur. Some kittens are born with a smudge of black hairs on top of their head. This is an indication that they will have normal hearing, at least in one ear. The spot disappears as the adult coat starts to grow at about nine months.

SHOW SUMMARY

The coat must be pure white throughout, with no shadow markings or black hairs. Nose-leather and paw pads are pink. Eyes deep blue; orange or copper; or one orange or copper and one deep blue. Pale or green tinged eyes are faults. 50 ▶

Below: A charming Black Persian with deep copper eyes.

BLACK PERSIAN

The Black Persian is a very old variety; it is one of nature's original breeds. It is still quite rare, however, probably because a perfect black is very difficult to obtain.

As with other black cats, the Persian is seen in some countries as a 'lucky' cat, notably in the United Kingdom; but in others it is considered 'unlucky' instead. As with other longhaired cats, Blacks were known in Europe at the end of the sixteenth century, but no one knows exactly where they came from, as there are no reliable early records. It can be said with certainty, however, that they first appeared on the British show bench in 1871. The early black cats were more like Angoras than Persians, with long noses and big ears, but these features have now been bred out, and the current champion will have the typical snub nose, round head and tiny ears.

Grooming

Daily grooming with brush and comb is essential. Bathing before a show may not be necessary, except to make the coat more fluffy, but the addition of bay rum to the coat will enhance the shine.

Do not use powder, as it will be impossible to brush it all out, and it will deaden the colour. Dampness and strong sunlight will produce a rusty tinge on the coat, so a show cat should be kept away from these two conditions whenever possible.

Breeding
Mating two Black Persians will produce black kittens, but to improve type it is also necessary to outcross to some of the other colours, notably Blue or White. In this case only the females from such crosses are used for further breeding. Black males from Black-to-Black matings are used to produce Tortoiseshells, Tortoiseshell-and-white (Calicos), Whites, Smokes, Creams and Bicolours.

Kittens
All kittens are born with blue eyes, which gradually change to copper. The kittens are born black but they often have rusty coats or some white hairs until the full adult jet black coat appears. In fact, the worst kitten coats at six months old often become the densest black adults at 12 to 18 months.

SHOW SUMMARY
The coat must be a solid even black all over, and each hair must be black from its tip down to its root. A real jet black is required, with no tinge of rustiness, no white hairs and no tabby markings. Noseleather and paw pads black. Eyes brilliant orange or deep copper. 50 ▶

BLUE PERSIAN

Blues have always been the most popular of the longhaired cats, with their long, flowing coats, delicate looks and sweet little faces.

It is said that they come from Persia (now Iran), Turkey, China, Burma, Afghanistan and Russia! They have featured in artists' impressions for several centuries, but they were largely unknown in

Above: A Blue Persian with lovely eyes and well-groomed coat.

Europe before the end of the sixteenth century. They were certainly known in Italy during the Renaissance, however, and were prized in India. First bred principally in France and England, where they enjoyed the patronage of Queen Victoria, they were later exported to the United States.

The blue colour is a dilution of black genetically, probably a result of crossing a black with a white cat originally, but blue cats did not appear in a separate class on the British show bench until 1889, although before that they may have been shown in mixed classes with Blue Tabbies and Blue-and-white Bicolours. Since hitting the show scene they have reigned supreme. They even have a show entirely to themselves in the United Kingdom, so numerous have they become.

Grooming
Daily grooming with brush and comb is essential. Bathing before a show is not usually necessary. Any grease marks can be removed by dusting the coat with grooming powder, taking care that it reaches the roots, and then brushing it well out.

Breeding
Blues are often used to produce Blue-creams and, because they seem to excel in Persian type, to improve the type of eye colour of other Persians.

Kittens

When born, the kittens may have tabby markings, but these usually disappear as the adult coat develops. In fact, the more heavily marked kittens often become the cats with the best all-over blue coats. The kittens are born with blue eyes, which change to deep orange over the next few months.

SHOW SUMMARY

The coat should be an even pale grey-blue all over, the same depth of colour from root to tip, with no sign of a paler undercoat and no tabby markings or white hairs. Generally the paler blue coats are preferred. Noseleather and paw pads slate blue. Eyes brilliant copper or deep orange with no green tinge. 51 ▶

RED PERSIAN

The Red Persian is an outstanding-looking cat with a flame-coloured, flowing coat. The name 'red' is misleading, as the coat colour is much more orange than scarlet,

more flame than crimson. Although red cats have appeared at shows since the beginning of the century, a really good specimen is very rare. In fact, it is almost impossible to produce without some tabby markings in the coat.

Grooming

Daily grooming is essential. Powder before a show or the application of a little bay rum will enhance the coat for a show appearance.

Breeding

Despite the predominance of male red cats (in the wild), red females do occur and can be obtained by mating a Red male with either a Tortoiseshell or a Blue-cream female (providing the male does not carry the blue colour factor in his genetic make-up). It is unwise to mate Reds to Red Tabbies, as this will reintroduce tabby markings. It is best to outcross to other self-

Below: A really fine looking Red Persian, which is quite different from the average 'ginger tom' found in domestic circles. It should have deep copper eyes.

coloured cats, such as Blacks. Reds are used to breed Tortoise-shells and Tortoiseshell-and-whites (Calicos).

Kittens
Red kittens are usually born with tabby markings, which they may or may not lose when the adult coat is grown. Often, therefore, it is difficult to tell whether there are Red or Red Tabby kittens in the litter, and breeding for Red Persians presents quite a challenge.

SHOW SUMMARY
The coat should be a deep, rich red without markings of any kind or white hairs. Noseleather and paw pads brick red. Eyes deep copper. 51 ▶

CREAM PERSIAN

Cream Persians are not as numerous as some of the other Persian varieties, perhaps because they have small litters as a rule. They are very beautiful cats and

quite ethereal-looking with their pale cream fur.

The Cream was first recorded in the United Kingdom in 1890, but at first such cats were generally regarded as Reds that were too pale to meet the show standard and many were sold as pets. Others were exported to the United States, where breeders have always been more interested in Cream Persians, and they are very popular there today. In the United Kingdom serious breeding for Creams in their own right did not start until the 1920s.

It is possible that Cream kittens first appeared in litters born to Tortoiseshells mated to Red Tabby males. Tortoiseshells have red, black and cream in their coats, and so this mating could produce some all-cream kittens. Any breeder who found this colour attractive could then proceed to isolate it by selective breeding.

Grooming
Daily grooming is essential. A bath may be necessary a few days before a show, and grooming powder will fluff the coat.

Breeding
Continuous like-to-like matings between Cream Persians produce gradual loss of type, and therefore outcrosses to other coloured varieties are necessary. Cream is genetically a dilution of the red colour and is, in fact, much easier to achieve than the solid red. Creams are produced most reliably from matings between Blues and Creams. A Cream female mated to a Blue male will produce Cream male and Blue-cream female kittens; a Cream male mated to a Blue female will produce Cream kittens of either sex, Blue males and Blue-cream females.

Kittens
Cream kittens are often born with faint tabby markings, but these usually disappear when the adult coat starts to develop at about nine months of age.

SHOW SUMMARY

The cream coat should be sound throughout, without markings of any kind and without a darker area down the spine. A medium depth of colour is preferred in the United Kingdom; American associations prefer a paler buff cream; too red ('hot') a colour is a fault. There should be no sign of a paler undercoat; the hair should be the same colour from root to tip. The coat colour may be darker in older cats or just before moulting. Nose-leather and paw pads pink. Eyes brilliant deep copper. 51 ▶

BICOLOUR PERSIAN

Two-coloured cats have been known since early times but are relative newcomers to the show bench, due to the fact that they were originally regarded as alley cats without known parentage. They can be Black-and-white, Blue-and-white, Red-and-white or Cream-and-white, although the latter are more rare. In pedigree breeding it has been difficult to meet the standard, which requires that the coat pattern should resemble that of the Dutch rabbit, with symmetrical patches of colour on the head and body; the symmetry seems to be an elusive characteristic, and few perfect Bicolours are seen. However, when achieved the cat is sure of adulation on the show bench. The 1979 Cat Fanciers' Association's Cat of the Year was in fact a Black-and-white female Persian of exceptional merit, which is no mean achievement in a country where the feline population exceeds 45 million (USA).

Grooming

Daily grooming is essential. For showing, a bath may be necessary, but powder should not be used on the coat as this tends to deaden the contrast between the colour and the white.

Breeding

Bicolours may be obtained from mating two Bicolours, a Bicolour with a Tortoiseshell-and-white, a Bicolour with a solid colour, or a solid colour with a White. They are accepted as being the best sires for producing Tortoiseshell-and-white kittens. Bicolour queens make excellent mothers, and the litters usually contain a colourful assortment of three or four kittens, of all the above patterns.

Kittens

Bicoloured kittens are robust and hardy and if kept for breeding can produce almost any coloured kitten, depending on their own ancestry and that of their mating partner. The kittens are large and mature early.

SHOW SUMMARY

The show Bicolour Persian must have a patched coat with not more than two-thirds of the body coloured and not more than one half white. The pattern should be symmetrical, with patches of colour on the face, head, back, flanks and tail. Accepted colours are Black-and-white (Magpie), Blue-and-white, Red-and-white and Cream-and-white (rare). Tabby markings and brindling (white hairs) within the colour patches are faults. White is desirable on the underparts, chest, feet, legs, chin and lips, and a facial blaze is preferred. A white collar is permitted. Noseleather and paw pads generally pink, otherwise in keeping with the coat colour. Eyes deep brilliant copper to orange in colour. 51 ▶

CHINCHILLA & SHELL CAMEO PERSIAN

The Persian Chinchillas and Cameos belong to a group that contains some of the most beautiful of all longhaired cats, which can

Above: This Blue-and-white Bicolour Persian shows both blue and pink noseleather.

conveniently be described as having a 'tipped' coat pattern. The characteristic feature of such cats is that the undercoat is one colour (usually white, but sometimes cream), and the guard hairs are tipped to varying extents with a different, contrasting colour. These cats are classified further according to whether the colour tipping is light (Chinchillas and Shell Cameos), medium (Shaded Silvers and Shaded Cameos) or heavy (Smokes).

In the Chinchillas and Shell Cameos, the undercoats are usually pure white, and the ends of some of the guard hairs, for approximately one-eighth of the hair length, are lightly tipped with a contrasting colour, giving a shimmering, sparkling effect to the coat.

The name Chinchilla is misleading, as the South American rodent whose name was given to this cat has fur that is dark at the roots and white at the tips — the opposite of the cat's coat. Despite this discrepancy, Chinchilla Persians have been so named since the 1890s, although the early Chinchillas were much more heavily marked, and probably rather more like today's Shaded Silvers. They are believed to have been developed from cats with silver genes, probably

Silver Tabbies, whose markings were indistinct or almost absent, mated to Blue Persians or Smokes; further selective breeding used only the palest kittens or non-tabby kittens mated to White Persians with blue eyes. Early Silver Tabbies would have had hazel or golden eyes, and the first Chinchillas also had hazel eyes; when these were mated to Blue-eyed White Persians, some of the kittens had green or blue-green eyes. These were considered an immediate success, and thereafter affected the standard. After the Second World War there was a shortage of all types of pedigree cats in Europe, and American Chinchillas were imported to improve the stamina of the variety. In Europe and Australia Chinchillas are, and have always been, fairy tale cats, finer-boned than other Persians, but in the United States, they are larger and conform more closely to the general Persian standard.

Their delicate appearance belies their hardy nature; they are not in fact fragile cats, but very robust and healthy. Their sweet baby faces and ethereal looks have made Chinchillas among the most popular of cats. Patronized before the Second World War by Queen Victoria's grand-daughter, Princess

Below: A Golden Chinchilla, one of the newest and most attractive Persian colour varieties.

Victoria, and being particularly photogenic, they are known worldwide, helped, no doubt, by their numerous appearances on television and in magazines.

Although the name Chinchilla traditionally conjures up a picture of a cat with a coat of black silk on white velvet, in recent years the name has been extended to cats of similar appearance and coat pattern but of different colour, notably the Chinchilla Golden, a lovely brown tipped variety now becoming popular in the United States and Europe.

The beautiful Shell Cameos are similar to the Chinchilla in coat pattern, and were developed in the late 1950s, mostly in the United States, by selective breeding of Silver Persians with Red cats. (In the United Kingdom, Creams were also used.) Using Chinchillas, the kittens were green-eyed, which was not desired, so Smokes with copper eyes were then introduced and mated to Reds or Tortoiseshells. In general, tabbies of any colour are not used (except to produce the Cameo Tabby), so as not to reintroduce any tabby markings. Such mixed breeding produces a wide variety of coloured Cameos, from the Red to the Tortoiseshell and the Blue-cream.

All Cameo varieties enjoyed immediate popularity because they are so beautiful, and they are now widely bred and appreciated in the United States, Europe, Australia and New Zealand.

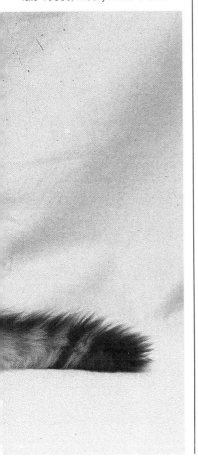

Grooming
For showing, Chinchillas and Cameos should be bathed a week before the show, then powdered with baby powder every day for four or five days to give back the body to the coat. Daily combing thereafter is essential to prevent the formation of knots. The day before the show, all traces of powder must be removed and each hair will stand out from the body. This is true show condition: every hair separate and the coat beautifully fluffy.

Sunlight affects the white fur and tends to give it a yellow tinge, so if showing the cat, try to keep it out of direct sunlight.

Breeding
Female Persians develop relatively slowly, and it is usually advisable not to arrange the first matings until the cats are 12 to 18 months old. This gives the females time to develop fully before bearing kittens. Once mated they usually become good mothers. To preserve the variety as it is, Chinchillas are now mated only to other Chinchillas, and it is advisable to mate the queen to a stud possessing all the qualities missing or less than perfect in the queen. For example,

19

if the queen has poor eye colour, a stud must be chosen that excels in the colour of his eyes.

Breeding for Cameos is more complex. First crosses of Copper-eyed Smokes to Red or Cream Persians preferably without blue in their backgrounds, or to Tortoiseshells, will produce Cameo males, which when mated to the Blue-cream, Tortoiseshell, Shaded Tortoiseshell or Shaded Blue-cream cats also produced from this mating, will give Shell Cameo females. Alternatively, Blue-cream and Tortoiseshell females can be mated to Red or Cream males. An exchange of blood lines (mating cats of different parents) will be better than brother and sister matings in some instances, if these can be found, and will also save waiting for two years until the kittens from the first mating mature.

The average Chinchilla and Cameo litter contains three or four kittens, though there was once a Chinchilla litter of 10.

Kittens

Chinchilla kittens are born with dark markings and tabby markings, particularly on the tail, but these disappear by the time they are four to six weeks old. If a kitten still shows markings after 10 weeks of age, then it is not destined for showing. Cameo kittens are born white, the tipping gradually appearing. They are particularly appealing when the colour develops, resembling balls of pink tinsel or vanilla ice-cream topped with orange sherbet!

SHOW SUMMARY

Chinchilla. Type to conform to the standard for Persians (United States), or to be slightly lighter boned and larger eared (United Kingdom). The undercoat should be pure white, the last one-eighth of each hair on the back, flanks, legs, head and tail tipped with black, giving a sparkling silver appearance to the coat. The chin, ear tufts, stomach and chest are pure white. The lips, nose and eyes

are outlined in black or deep brown. Whiskers should be white, but may be black nearest the face. Noseleather brick red: a pale noseleather is considered a fault. Paw pads black. Eyes emerald green to blue-green. 52 ▶

Masked Silver Persian. A Chinchilla with a pure white undercoat and top coat tipped lightly with black on the back, flanks and tail, but with darker, heavier tipping on the face and paws. Noseleather brick red. Paw pads black or deep brown. Eyes green or blue-green.

Below: A lovely Shell Cameo (Red Chinchilla) Persian with dainty red tipping on white.

Chinchilla Golden. The undercoat should be a rich, warm cream. The coat on the back, flanks, head and tail is lightly tipped with seal brown to give a sparkling golden appearance. The legs may be very lightly tipped. The chin, ear tufts, stomach and chest should be cream. The lips, nose and eyes should be outlined with seal brown. Noseleather deep rose. Paw pads seal brown. Eyes green or blue-green.

Shell Cameo. (Red Chinchilla). The undercoat should be pure white with the coat on the back, flanks, legs and tail lightly tipped with red (and/or cream in United Kingdom) to give an enchanting sparkling pink tinsel effect. The chin, ear tufts, stomach and chest are pure white. Tabby markings are a fault. Noseleather and paw pads rose. Eyes brilliant copper, outlined in rose. 52 ▸

Shell Tortoiseshell. (Tortoiseshell Cameo, Tortie-cream Cameo). This colouring is a female only variety currently. The undercoat should be pure white, lightly tipped with red, black and cream in well-defined patches, and well broken on the face. The chin, ear tufts, stomach and chest are white. A blaze of red or cream tipping on the face is desirable. Noseleather and paw pads black, pink or a combination of the two. Eyes brilliant copper.

Blue-cream Particolour Cameo.
Females only. The undercoat
should be pure white. The coat on
the back, flanks, legs and tail is
lightly tipped with blue and cream,
softly intermingled, to give the effect
of a mantle of mother of pearl.
Noseleather and paw pads blue,
pink or a combination of the two.
Eyes deep copper.

Cameo Tabby. Undercoat should
be off-white, lightly tipped with red
in either classic or mackerel tabby
coat pattern. Noseleather and paw
pads rose. Eyes brilliant copper. 52 ▶

SHADED PERSIAN

Similar to the Chinchillas and Shell
Cameos, the Shaded Persians also
have pale (usually white) undercoats, but approximately a quarter
of the hair length is tipped with a
contrasting colour to give the effect
of a coloured mantle over the body.

Shaded kittens appear in the
same litters as Chinchillas and
Cameos, and the information given
about breeding also applies to the

*Above: A Shaded Silver Persian
with white undercoat and heavier
black tipping than the Chinchilla.*

Shaded Persians (see pages 19-20).
In the early days of pedigree cat
breeding, when Chinchillas were
darker than they are today, it was
difficult to distinguish between the
two types. It is only recently that
interest in the shaded cats has been
revived and a standard introduced
for them. They are very much loved
in the United States and Australia
and are now bred in several
colours, although the original
variety was Silver. There is no
reason why, with well-regulated
outcrossing to other coloured
Persians, they should not be bred
in any coat colour or pattern.

Grooming
Daily grooming is essential. Show
preparation requires the same
treatment as for Chinchillas and
Shell Cameos.

SHOW SUMMARY
Shaded Silver. The undercoat
should be pure white, the top coat
tipped in black to give the effect of
a black mantle overlying the
undercoat, on the back, flanks,

face, legs and tail. Generally darker than the Chinchilla. Noseleather and paw pads brick red. Eyes green or blue-green, rimmed in black. 53▶

Shaded Cameo. (Red Shaded). The undercoat should be pure white, with the top coat tipped in red to give the effect of a red mantle overlying the undercoat, on the back, flanks, face, legs and tail. Generally darker than the Shell Cameo. Noseleather and paw pads rose. Eyes brilliant copper, rimmed with rose. 53▶

Shaded Golden. The undercoat should be a rich, warm cream, with the top coat tipped in seal brown to give the effect of a golden overcoat. Generally darker than the Chinchilla Golden. Noseleather deep rose. Paw pads seal brown. Eyes green or blue-green, rimmed in seal brown.

Shaded Tortoiseshell. The undercoat should be pure white, with the top coat tipped in black, red and cream in well-defined patches of the tortoiseshell pattern. Generally much darker than the Shell Tortoiseshell. A blaze of red or cream on the face is desirable. Noseleather and paw pads black, pink, or a combination of the two. Eyes brilliant copper.

Pewter. The undercoat should be white, with the top coat tipped in black, giving the effect of a black mantle overlying the undercoat. Generally darker than the Chinchilla but similar to the Shaded Silver. Lips, nose and eyes outlined in black. Noseleather brick red. Paw pads black. Eyes orange or copper, with no green tinge.

SMOKE PERSIAN

Like the Chinchillas and Shaded Persians, the Smokes are also characterized by their white undercoats and contrasting tipped top coats. But these hairs are tipped for at least half their length with colour and at first glance, Smoke Persians may look like solid-coloured cats until they move, when the beautiful pale undercoat shows through. The ruff and ear tufts are generally of the paler colour, making these cats among the most striking of the Persians.

Smoke-coloured cats have been recorded in the United Kingdom since the 1860s, and appeared originally as the result of chance matings of Chinchilla, Black, Blue, and White Persians. Very good Smokes were shown in England in the first 20 years of this century, but then, oddly, their popularity declined, until interest was revived again in the 1960s. Now several colours are being bred, but so far not all are recognized for competition in all countries.

Grooming
More than most varieties, Smoke Persians require frequent and expert grooming to look their best. In fact, it may take many weeks of dedication before the contrasting coat is ready to be shown to perfection.

Apart from a bath a week before the show to remove grease, the undercoat must be well brushed up to show through the dark top coat. This is a job that requires patience and skill; too much brushing may pull out the undercoat. Strong sunlight tends to bleach the coat, so Smokes are best shown during the winter months.

Breeding
Outcrosses to improve type can be made to Black, Blue or Tortoiseshell Persians, giving Black, Blue or Tortoiseshell Smokes; this will preserve the copper eyes. Silver Tabbies should not be used, because they would reintroduce the green eye and tabby markings, neither of which is desirable, although there was a time in the United Kingdom when green eyes were permitted. Another good cross is to a Chinchilla, to improve

the undercoat, though again this may introduce the green eye colour.

In order to produce all-Smoke kittens, the parents must have a Smoke in their backgrounds; but Black is dominant over Smoke, and therefore Black-to-Smoke matings will produce all-Black kittens. Even Smoke-to-Smoke matings may produce some all-Black kittens. Unfortunately mating Smokes with Smokes repeatedly results in loss of Persian type.

Kittens

Smokes are difficult to distinguish at birth from their solid-coloured counterparts, except that Smoke kittens sometimes have white around the eyes and a paler stomach. It may take some months to distinguish which will be Smokes, and the full coat colour and pattern is sometimes not seen until the adult coat is grown at about two years of age. Kittens whose undercoats get paler quickest usually become the best adult Smokes. The undercoat begins to show through at about three weeks, and by six to eight weeks old the cats have a mottled appearance. At six months they are ready to be shown. Kittens with unsatisfactory coats can be sold as pets and will make affectionate, even-tempered companions.

SHOW SUMMARY

Black Smoke. The undercoat should be white, heavily tipped on the back and flanks with black to give the effect of a solid coloured cat, until the animal moves. The coat shades to silver on the lower

Below: The Black Smoke Persian has a white undercoat with heavy black tipping and lustrous eyes.

flanks. The face and feet are black, with no markings (colour solid to the roots in the United Kingdom; white at the roots in the United States). The ruff and ear tufts are silver. Noseleather and paw pads black. Eyes brilliant copper or orange.

Blue Smoke. The undercoat should be white, heavily tipped with blue on the back and flanks to give the appearance of a solid blue cat, until the animal moves. The face and feet are blue, without markings (colour solid to the roots in the United Kingdom; white at the roots in the United States). The ruff and ear tufts are silver. Noseleather and paw pads blue. Eyes brilliant orange or copper. 53 ▶

Cameo Smoke. (Red Smoke). The undercoat should be white, heavily tipped with red on the back and

flanks to give the appearance of a solid red cat, until the animal moves. The face and feet are red, without markings (colour solid to the roots in the United Kingdom; white at the roots in the United States). The ruff and ear tufts are white. Noseleather and paw pads rose. Eyes brilliant orange or copper.

Smoke Tortoiseshell. The undercoat should be white, heavily tipped with black, red and cream in clearly defined patches on the back and flanks to give the appearance of a tortoiseshell cat, until the animal moves. Face and feet solid red, black and cream, with preference given to a facial blaze of red or cream. (Colours solid to the roots in the United Kingdom; white at the roots in the United States.) Ruff and ear tufts white. Noseleather and paw pads charcoal, rose, pink or a combination of these colours. Eyes brilliant copper.

TORTOISESHELL PERSIAN

Despite the fact that tortoiseshell shorthaired cats have been domesticated in Europe since the days of the Roman Empire, the longhaired Tortoiseshell was not recorded before the end of the nineteenth century.

Tortoiseshells first appeared at cat shows in the early 1900s, and became popular on both sides of the Atlantic, although because they are difficult to breed, they are still relatively rare. As a result, the demand for a Tortoiseshell kitten invariably exceeds the supply and they may be more expensive than other Persians.

Grooming
Daily grooming with brush and comb throughout the year is essential to keep the coat in good condition. Grooming powder should not be used as it will deaden the colour.

Breeding

As this is a female-only variety, and the rare male seems invariably sterile, like-to-like mating is not possible and breeding is difficult and unpredictable. Mating Tortoise-shells to various self-coloured males — Black, Blue, Red or Cream — or to Bicolours cannot be relied upon to produce a single Tortoise-shell kitten! It is more by luck that one appears as an occasional kitten in a litter. Tabby sires should not be used as they would introduce unwanted bars and markings.

Kittens

When Tortoiseshells are mated to males of different colours, a very colourful assortment of kittens usually results, and they are not difficult to find homes for.

SHOW SUMMARY

The coat should be evenly patched with red, cream and black. All colours should be clear and brilliant rather than mingled. Black should not predominate, and over-large patches of any one colour are considered a fault. A red or cream blaze from the forehead to the nose is desirable. The colours should be well broken up on the head and ears and the fur should be particularly long on the ruff and tail. White hairs and tabby markings are faults. Noseleather and paw pads pink or black. Eyes copper or deep orange. 54 ▶

BLUE-CREAM PERSIAN

The Blue-cream is a female-only variety, genetically a dilute form of the Tortoiseshell, and a most attractive and popular cat. Although relatively slow to gain championship status, achieving official recognition in the United Kingdom only in 1930, they had appeared in litters resulting from Blue and Cream matings ever since pedigree cat breeding began, and were first shown in the United States as Blue Tortoiseshells in the early 1900s.

It is now generally recognized that they are very valuable as breeding stock for Blues, Creams and Blue-creams. The crossing of two longhaired varieties has given stamina to both Blues and Creams and the Blue-creams themselves are a very healthy and robust variety of good Persian type.

The British and American standards are quite different. The former calls for evenly intermingled blue and cream throughout the coat, but the latter requires well-broken patches of blue and cream.

Grooming

Daily grooming with brush and comb is essential. A bath may be necessary before a show, and a little grooming powder to fluff the coat into show condition.

Breeding

If a Blue-cream is mated to a Cream sire, the resulting kittens will be everything except Blue females. If a Blue-cream is mated to a Blue sire, the resulting kittens will be everything except cream females. Similarly, a Blue female mated to a Cream male will produce Blue-cream female and Blue male kittens, whereas a Blue male mated to a Cream female will produce Blue-cream female and Cream male kittens.

Kittens

The kittens are very pretty and colourful, and there may be Blues, Creams and Blue-creams in any litter. Those with the palest coats will probably develop into the best adults from a competition point of view. Often a very fine Blue-cream will look much like pale blue in the first few weeks, so breeding Blue-creams can be quite exciting.

SHOW SUMMARY

The British standard dictates that the coat should be evenly coloured in pastel shades of blue and cream, softly intermingled throughout; the

American standard requires the coat to be blue patched with solid cream, clearly defined and well broken on body, legs, tail and face. Noseleather and paw pads blue or pink or a combination. Eyes deep copper or orange. 54 ▶

TORTOISESHELL -AND-WHITE PERSIAN (Calico)

The Tortoiseshell-and-white (Calico) Persian is another female-only variety, with a delightfully patched coat of black, red and cream with white. Beautiful cats, they are always in demand.

Although shorthaired Tortoiseshell-and-white cats have been known in Europe for centuries, the origin of the longhaired variety is obscure. Like the Tortoiseshell, it is

Above: The Blue-cream Persian (UK) has a mingled coat of blue and cream with lustrous copper eyes. A healthy and robust variety.

said to have no distinct history, and probably arose by chance in litters of solid-coloured Persians with mixed colour backgrounds.

The colour is sex-linked genetically to produce females only, and when the rare male occurs, it is invariably sterile. Cats with this coat pattern were known in the past as 'chintz' cats, because of the bright, bold colour patches.

On the show bench, the pedigree variety is relatively new, attaining recognition only in the 1950s. More recently, the dilute variety, Blue Tortoiseshell-and-white (Dilute Calico), has also attained recognition in Europe and the United States. Such cats often appear in the same litter as Tortoiseshell-and-whites, and have patched coats of blue and cream with white.

In the United Kingdom, the standard requires the colour patches to be interspersed with white, but in the United States, the preference is for white to be concentrated on the underparts. One American association describes the cat as a Tortoiseshell that has been dropped into a pail of milk, the milk having splashed up onto the face and neck.

Grooming

This cat's coat is said not to mat as much as most Persian varieties, but a daily brushing and combing is still advisable. If it is being prepared for a show, a little Fuller's earth can be rubbed into the lighter parts of the coat and then thoroughly brushed out.

Breeding

Like Tortoiseshells, Tortoiseshell-and-whites are also renowned for producing kittens in a lovely assortment of colours, but it appears that more Tortoiseshell-and-white kittens are born when sired by Red-and-white or Black-and-white Bicoloured cats. Those producing the best patched coats are males with too much white in their own coats, according to the Bicolour standard. Tabbies should not be used as they might introduce bars and markings, which are rather undesirable.

Kittens

The kittens often have patches of dull blue, dark cream or drab white when young, but these usually turn into jet black, bright red and pure white patches in the adult. Blue Tortoiseshell-and-white kittens, which often appear in the same litter, are generally paler in colour. In both cases, however, it is difficult to assess the quality of the coat colouring when the kittens are young.

SHOW SUMMARY
Tortoiseshell-and-white (Calico). The cat should be strikingly. patched with black, red and cream, interspersed with white. The

patches should be equally distributed, bright and clear, without white hairs (brindling) or tabby markings, and should be evenly spread over the body with white on the legs, feet, chest and face. Too much white is a fault. The American standard requires white to be concentrated on the underparts. A cream or white blaze from the top of the head to the nose is desirable, especially when it sharply divides the black side of the face from the red side. Nose-leather and paw pads pink, black or a combination of the two. Eyes brilliant copper. 54 ▶

Blue Tortoiseshell-and-white

(Dilute Calico). Coat should be patched with blue and cream. Patches should be evenly distributed over the body, clear and unbrindled, with white on the legs, feet, chest and face, and concentrated on the underparts (US). A cream or white blaze on the face is desirable. Noseleather and paw pads pink. Eyes brilliant copper or orange.

CHOCOLATE TORTOISESHELL & LILAC-CREAM PERSIAN

New varieties developed from the Colourpoint (Himalayan) breeding programme, with outcrossing to Tortoiseshell and Cream Persians respectively. In the United States they are regarded as Himalayan hybrids (see page 39) and cannot be shown. In the UK, however, they have received official recognition as varieties of Persian (Longhair).

SHOW SUMMARY
Chocolate Tortoiseshell. The coat should be patched with chocolate, red and cream. The colours should be bright and rich, and well broken on the face. Noseleather and paw pads brown. Eyes copper.

Above: A Blue Tortoiseshell-and-white has blue, cream and white markings and large orange eyes.

Lilac-cream. Throughout the coat shades of lilac and cream should be softly intermingled, with no white hairs. Noseleather and paw pads pink. Eyes copper.

TABBY PERSIAN

Persian Tabby cats are creatures of great beauty. They make excellent pets for people who have the time to devote to their grooming and well-being. Generally they are healthy, docile and rather more independent and outdoor loving than other Persian varieties.

The name 'tabby' is said to have come originally from the similarity of the cat's coat pattern to tabby or plain woven watered silk or taffeta, which was known as tabbisilk in England. This type of weaving produces a striped or ridged effect on the cloth. The word itself probably derives from Attabiya, a district in Baghdad where this material was made.

The tabby pattern is very common among domestic cats, although longhaired tabbies were not recorded in Europe until the end of the sixteenth century. Judging from the markings of many wild felines, the original domestic tabby was probably a striped cat, resembling the Mackeral Tabby of today. It appears that the classic or blotched pattern, more common now in pedigree cats, is a mutation of the striped form that first appeared in Europe among domestic and feral cats and was already common by the middle of the seventeenth century.

Although the original tabby colours are likely to have been brown and red, or rather, ginger, selective breeding over the last 100 years has produced several others, of which the striking Brown Tabby is not a common variety in pedigree circles, possibly because it is extremely difficult to breed a cat to the required colour standard. Affectionately known as 'brownies', they are noted for their health, strength and longevity, and deserve a larger following.

The Red Tabbies are particularly popular in the United States, as are the Silver Tabbies, which always attract attention at shows in all countries. Silver Tabbies were bred in the United States long before there were organized cat shows.

The Blue Tabby is a variety more recently recognized for competition in the United States and

Europe. As blue is a dilution of black genetically, kittens with this colouring appear from time to time in Brown Tabby litters, especially if there is a blue cat in the ancestry.

The clearly defined tabby markings required by the show standards are difficult to achieve in all the tabbies, but especially so in the Cream Tabby. Genetically a dilute form of the Red, it shows very little contrast between the ground colour and the markings, and as a result a good specimen is rare. This variety is recognized for competition in the USA only, at present.

Grooming

To show a Tabby Persian to perfection the coat must be brushed to enhance the markings. This entails brushing and combing only from head to tail, with no forward brushing to fluff up the coat as can be done with some of the self-coloured varieties. The use of powder on the coat is not recommended as it tends to deaden the contrast between the ground colour and the markings. Some bay rum to remove grease is beneficial before a show.

Breeding

Mating two Tabbies of the required colour together will give several generations of good type but eventually outcrossing to a solid colour will be necessary, using in each case the solid colour of the overlay coat pattern, or, alternatively, a Tortoiseshell. Thus in the Brown Tabby, this will mean an outcross to a solid Black Persian; in the Red Tabby to a Red or a Tortoiseshell; in the Silver Tabby to a Black; in the Blue Tabby to a Blue Persian; and in the Cream Tabby to a Cream. In the case of the Silver Tabby this may introduce the golden eye colour, which is undesirable, and consequently a Chinchilla can be used.

Kittens

Tabby kittens are very colourful balls of fluff, with the markings showing even as they are being born. Often the darker striped they are at birth, the clearer the adult coat pattern will be. Imperfectly marked kittens unsuitable for showing will make excellent colourful pets. These include those with white hairs in the darker markings, white patches, a white tip to the tail or a white chin, too solid a colour down the back and incorrect eye colour; also, in Silver Tabbies a brown or yellow tinge to the fur.

SHOW SUMMARY

Classic Tabby pattern. All markings should be clearly defined from the ground colour. The characteristic head marking is a letter 'M' resembling frown marks on the forehead. Unbroken lines run from the outer corners of the eyes towards the back of the head. There are other pencil-thin lines on the face, especially in the form of swirls on the cheeks. Lines extend back from the top of the head to the shoulder markings, which are shaped in a butterfly pattern. Three unbroken lines run parallel to each other down the spine from the shoulder markings to the base of the tail. A large blotch on each flank is circled by one or more unbroken rings; these markings should be symmetrical on either side of the body. There should be several unbroken necklaces on the neck and upper chest, and a double row of 'buttons' running from chest to stomach. Both legs and tail should be evenly ringed.

Mackerel Tabby pattern. (Rare in Persians, but recognized in the United States.) Head is marked with the characteristic 'M', and there is an unbroken line running from the outer corner of the eyes towards the back of the head. There are other fine pencil markings on the cheeks. A narrow unbroken line runs from the back of the head to the base of the tail. The rest of the body is marked with narrow unbroken lines running vertically down from the spine line. These lines should be as narrow

and numerous as possible and, ideally, clearly defined from the ground colour. There should be several unbroken necklaces on the neck and upper chest, and a double row of 'buttons' on the chest and stomach. The legs should be evenly barred with narrow bracelets and the tail evenly ringed.

Brown Tabby. Ground colour rich tawny sable to coppery brown. Markings jet black. No white hairs. Noseleather brick red. Paw pads black or dark brown, the dark colour extending up the backs of the hind legs from paw to heel. Eyes brilliant copper or hazel. 55 ▶

Red Tabby. Ground colour rich red. Markings dark rich red. Lips and chin red. No white hairs or patches. Noseleather brick red. Paw pads pink. Eyes brilliant copper or gold. 55 ▶

Silver Tabby. Ground silver. Markings jet black and clearly defined. Noseleather brick red. Paw pads black. Eyes green or hazel. 55 ▶

Blue Tabby. Ground colour, lips and chin pale bluish ivory. Markings very deep slate blue. Noseleather deep rose pink. Paw pads rose pink. Eyes brilliant copper.

Cream Tabby. Ground colour, lips and chin very pale cream. Markings rich cream, not too red, but sufficiently dark to afford a contrast with the ground colour. Nose-

Above: A Blue Tabby Persian with brilliant copper eyes. Long hair distorts the true tabby coat.

leather and paw pads pink. Eyes brilliant copper.

Cameo Tabby. Ground colour, lips and chin off white. Markings red. Noseleather and paw pads rose. Eyes brilliant copper to gold.

Patched Tabby (Torbie) pattern. Markings classic or mackerel tabby with red and/or cream patches. Facial blaze preferred.
Brown. Ground colour coppery brown. Markings jet black, with red and/or cream. Noseleather brick red. Paw pads black or brown. Eyes brilliant copper.
Silver. Ground colour pale silver. Markings jet black with red and/or cream. Noseleather and paw pads rose pink. Eyes copper or hazel.
Blue. Ground colour pale bluish ivory. Markings deep slate blue with red and/or cream. Eyes brilliant copper.

VAN PERSIANS

Mostly white cats with patches of colour on head, legs and tail. Noseleather and paw pads in keeping with coat colour or pink. Eyes copper/gold.
Van Bicolour. Patches of black, blue, red or cream.
Van Calico. Patches of black/red.
Van Blue-cream. Patches of blue and cream.

PEKE-FACED PERSIAN

Good points
- *Affectionate*
- *Intelligent*
- *Quiet*
- *Suitable for an apartment*
- *Companionable*

Take heed
- *Needs daily grooming*
- *May suffer breathing difficulties*
- *May have feeding problems*

From time to time in Red Self and Red Tabby Persian litters, there appears spontaneously a different-looking kitten with a face resembling that of a Pekingese dog. Such a cat has a much shorter nose and an obvious indentation between the eyes, and because of this is known as a Peke-faced Persian. It is just as sweet and companionable as other Persians, but because of its very large jowls and very snub nose, it may suffer from snuffles and other breathing problems, and also from feeding problems if the upper and lower teeth do not meet in an even bite.

Although the Peke-faced Persian has appeared occasionally else-where, at present it is virtually unknown outside the United States.

Grooming
Like all Persians, the Peke-faced requires daily grooming with brush and comb to remove knots and tangles from the long coat. Attention must also be paid to the eyes, as the tear ducts may become blocked. Any mucus that collects in the corners of the eyes should be sponged away with warm water. The ears and teeth should be examined regularly.

Origin and history
Peke-faced Persians have been bred in the United States for many years. They have been shown there since the 1930s, and are popular cats. However, the breed has attracted criticism, especially from veterinarians, because its extreme characteristics may cause breathing and feeding difficulties.

Breeding
Two Peke-faced cats mated to-gether do not necessarily produce Peke-faced kittens. The best ones come from Red Tabby and Peke-faced matings.

It is not immediately obvious whether there are any Peke-faced kittens in a litter of Red Selfs or Red Tabbies, as the characteristics do not show for some weeks. Special care has to be taken by breeders to make sure that the extreme physical features that are known to cause problems are reduced, as it is these features that have limited the breed's popularity in the past.

Kittens
There is a high mortality rate among Peke-faced kittens due to the difficulties encountered in feeding and breathing in cats with extremely snub noses (over-typed). The kittens often try to feed with their paws, bringing the food to their mouths. If they do not have an even bite, they may not be able to get enough to eat. They develop slowly and seem to remain kittens for longer than other Persians.

Kittens with just sufficient facial characteristics to be recognized as Peke-faced, but without the problems associated with over-typing, develop normally.

SHOW SUMMARY
The Peke-faced Persian is a solid, cobby cat of Persian type, but with a

Right: A characteristic Red Tabby Peke-faced Persian. These cats are quiet and companionable, adapting well to apartment life.

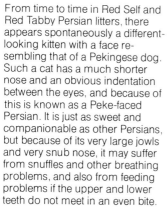

distinctive face, which resembles that of a Pekingese dog.

Coat. Long, flowing, silky and soft with a large ruff around the neck.

Body. Short, cobby and massive. Legs short. Paws large and well tufted.

Tail. Short, well plumed and especially full at the base.

Head. Large, round and heavy with a very short snub nose, indented between the eyes, giving an obvious nose break. The muzzle is wrinkled and there is a fold of skin running from the corner of the eye to the mouth. The forehead bulges out above the nose and eyes. The neck is short and thick. The ears are small, although slightly larger than other Persians.

Eyes. Very prominent, almost bulging, round and full.

PEKE-FACED COLOURS

Only two colours are recognized for competition at present, although Peke-faced cats also appear in dilute red (cream).

Red. Body colour an even deep, rich red throughout with no markings or white hairs. Noseleather and paw pads brick red. Eyes brilliant copper.

Red Tabby. Ground colour red. Markings, in either classic or mackerel tabby pattern, deep rich red. Noseleather and paw pads brick red. Eyes brilliant copper.56 ▶

RAGDOLL

Good points
- Gentle and affectionate
- Quiet
- Playful
- Intelligent
- Suitable for an apartment

Take heed
- Vulnerable
- Has a high tolerance of pain
- Needs daily grooming

The Ragdoll is a large cuddly cat and fun to have around. It has lots of fur, which is said not to mat. It is a quiet, loyal and affectionate cat and very dependent on its owner. Because it is supposed not to feel pain, the Ragdoll is vulnerable and any injury may go unnoticed. Anyone contemplating owning a Ragdoll should therefore expect to be entirely responsible for it, as this cat, more than any other, requires mothering.

The Ragdoll has another unique feature: when picked up and carried it relaxes completely, becoming limp like a ragdoll or bean bag. Although this has given the breed its name and a large press coverage, scientific tests have shown that, physiologically, this cat is no different from others.

Grooming
Because the Ragdoll has a very long coat, it will need daily grooming, if not to remove knots and tangles, then to remove dead hairs. As it moults heavily in the summer, thorough grooming at this time is particularly important. The tangles should be combed out using a wide-toothed comb, then the coat brushed gently but thoroughly using a long-bristled brush.

Origin and history
The Ragdoll originated in California and its ancestors are very mixed. The foundation stock seems to have involved a white Angora, a Birman and a non-pedigree Burmese. This mixed blood has resulted in large and vigorous descendants. Within the accepted

Above: A Colourpoint Seal-point Ragdoll. One of the newest breeds.

colours, Ragdolls breed true, so that today Ragdolls are mated only to Ragdolls, although in the early days of the breed there were many back crosses to the foundation sires. The breed was first recognized for competition in the United States in 1965. At present Ragdolls are unknown outside the USA.

Breeding
To preserve the distinguishing features of the breed, Ragdolls are mated only to Ragdolls. It is possible to produce Ragdoll kittens in one of the desired coat patterns and colours in every litter.

Kittens
Like all Himalayan-patterned cats, the kittens are born all-white, the point colours and coat shading developing gradually. Ragdoll kittens are slow to mature and it may be three years before the full adult coat is developed.

SHOW SUMMARY
The Ragdoll is a large, heavily built

cat with a long flowing coat and a characteristic limpness when held.

Coat. Exceptionally long, full and silky. Non-matting. Luxuriant ruff and extra-long fur on the chest and stomach; shorter on the face. The coat is likely to be longer in cold than in warm climates and will moult considerably during the summer months.

Body. Very large and heavy with strong heavy bones. Males 6.8-9kg (15-20lb); females 4-5.4kg (9-12lb) and shorter in body than males. Hindquarters are heavy and there is a furry loose-muscled stomach pad. As broad across the shoulders as across the rump, with a deep chest. Legs medium in length and fairly heavy with hind legs slightly longer than forelegs. Paws large, round and firm with tufts between the toes.

Tail. Long and furry. Medium thick at the base with a slight taper towards the tip. A short or kinked tail would be a fault.

Head. Medium in size with a modified wedge; wider in the male than in the female. The skull between the ears is flat. The cheeks are full and taper to a full round chin. There is a gentle nose break, which, with the flat head, gives a distinctive profile. Neck is strong, short and thick. Ears are medium in size, broad at the base, tilted forward, rounded at the tips and furnished with ear tufts. Very large, very small or pointed ears are faults.

Eyes. Very large, oval, set wide apart. Round or almond-shaped eyes or squints are faults.

RAGDOLL COLOURS

Ragdolls are bred in three coat patterns — colourpoint, mitted and bicolour — and in seal, chocolate, blue and lilac point colours within these patterns. All are recognized for competition in the United States.

Colourpoint. Body colour should be an even shade down to the roots. Points (ears, mask, legs and tail) darker providing a distinct contrast with the body colour. Chest, bib and chin a much lighter shade of the body colour. Ticking and white spotting not accepted.

Mitted. Body colour should be an even shade down to the roots. Points (ears, mask, legs and tail) darker, providing a distinct contrast with the body colour. Chest, bib and chin white. A white stripe runs from the bib between the forelegs to the base of the tail. White mittens on both front paws should be evenly matched and scalloped. White boots on hind legs also to match. Coloured spots in white areas or ticking on coloured areas are faults.

Bicolour. Body colour should be an even shade down to the roots. The ears, mask (with the exception of an inverted 'V' down the nose, which is white) and tail are darker and clearly defined. Chest, stomach and legs white. The symmetrical inverted 'V' on the face starts between the ears, covers the nose, whisker pads, neck and bib. It should not extend beyond the outer edge of the eyes. There should be no coloured spots on the white areas. The body areas may have small spots of white. 56 ▸

Seal-point. Body colour a pale fawn shading to pale cream on the underparts. Points dense seal brown. Noseleather dark brown. Paw pads dark brown or black. Eyes deep blue.

Chocolate-point. Body colour an even ivory all over. Points warm milk-chocolate. Noseleather rose. Paw pads salmon. Eyes deep blue.

Blue-point. Body colour an even platinum grey-blue, shading to lighter blue on the underparts. Points deep blue-grey. Noseleather and paw pads dark blue-grey. Eyes deep blue.

Lilac-(Frost-) point. Body colour an even milk white all over. Points frosty grey-pink. Inside ears very pale pink. Noseleather lilac. Paw pads coral pink. Eyes deep blue.

COLOURPOINT (Himalayan)

Good points
- *Beautiful*
- *Affectionate*
- *Devoted*
- *Intelligent*
- *Quick to learn*
- *Good with children*

Take heed
- *Needs daily grooming*
- *Does not like to be caged*

A Colourpoint is essentially a Persian with Siamese (Himalayan) colouring. It is rather more demanding and more enterprising than many of the Persians, although more docile and less demonstrative than the Siamese. As with all cats, the Colourpoint likes to choose its own activities and will be happiest if given the run of the house or garden.

It would not be advisable to have a Colourpoint as a pet unless you are prepared to devote a lot of time to its grooming. Well cared for, the Colourpoint, or 'Himmy' as it is affectionately known, is an extremely beautiful cat, and makes a very affectionate and devoted pet.

Show cats will be expensive but kittens that do not quite meet the standard for showing can be obtained more reasonably and will make excellent and charming companions just the same.

Grooming
As for all longhaired cats, daily grooming is essential for the Colourpoint. If neglected, the undercoat will become matted into tight knots that in an extreme case might have to be cut out under anaesthetic. Despite regular attention mats do sometimes form, particularly if the cat spends a lot of time outside, and in experienced hands a mat cutter, designed for dogs, can be used to cut through a mat to remove it rather than cutting it out and leaving a bare spot. But be careful not to cut the cat!

A wide-toothed comb can be used to remove knots, followed by a medium-toothed comb to

remove dead hairs. Finally, the coat should be brushed with a long-handled, pure-bristle brush. Repeated daily, this will ensure a healthy coat and the cat will enjoy the process. A little dry grooming powder dusted into the coat before brushing will usually help to untangle the fur, but it should be brushed out thoroughly afterwards. Inspection of the eyes for blocked tear ducts and the ears for mites completes the daily routine.

Origin and history
The Colourpoint or Himalayan is a 'manufactured' breed, specifically produced by breeders. It is not a Siamese with long hair, but a Persian with Siamese (Himalayan) colouring. The name Himalayan derives from the coat pattern of the Himalayan rabbit, where the darker colour is confined to the face, legs and tail (as in the Siamese), and not because of any pretensions to a Himalayan origin, geographically. Its production involved complex scientific breeding and took years to perfect into the correct Persian type. Breeders had been crossing Siamese with Persians for many years but had been getting only self-coloured shorthaired kittens as a result. Eventually, in the 1940s, a series of scientific experiments was made, crossing Siamese with longhaired Blacks and Blues. The resulting shorthaired self-coloured kittens proved very useful for breeding as they carried the genes required to produce the Colourpoint. They were mated together and back to their parents until Colourpoint kittens were pro-

duced. Further selective breeding back to longhaired Blacks and Blues to develop Persian type was carried out and the resulting cats, when mated back to Colourpoints, produced excellent, new generation Colourpoints. Eventually, after 10 years of selective breeding, the long noses and large ears of the Siamese were bred out, but the Himalayan coat pattern, blue eyes and Persian type were fixed, and the lovely Colourpoints had arrived. The breed was recognized for competition in 1955 in the United Kingdom, and independently as the Himalayan in the United States in 1957.

Breeding

Colourpoint-to-Colourpoint breeding produces 100 percent Colourpoint kittens, but to preserve type, outcrosses are still made to self-coloured Persians and the offspring mated back to the original Colourpoints. With outcrossing to other coloured Persians, all point colours are possible. The mixed breeding has rendered the Colourpoint a particularly hardy breed, and litters containing six kittens are not uncommon.

Below: A really beautiful Seal-point Colourpoint Persian showing large blue eyes set wide apart.

Kittens

The kittens are born with creamy white fur and pink paw pads, noses and ears. The point colouration gradually develops over the first few weeks. They are charming little balls of fluff with plenty of energy and enterprise.

SHOW SUMMARY

The Colourpoint (Himalayan) is essentially a Persian-type cat, although slightly larger, with the Himalayan coat pattern: the main colour is confined to the mask, legs and tail. The British standard has been accepted for all countries.
Coat. Long, thick, soft and silky, standing well away from the body. The ruff is very full and extends to a frill between the front legs.
Body. Cobby and low on the legs. Deep in the chest. Massive across the shoulders and rump, and short and rounded in between. Long, svelte Siamese lines are a fault. The legs are short and thick, straight and strong. The paws are large, round and firm with long toe tufts.
Tail. Short, very full and carried low. A long or kinked tail is a fault.
Head. Broad and round with width between the ears. The neck is short, and thick. The face is well rounded. The nose is short and broad with a definite nose break in profile. The ears are small, rounded

at the tips, tilted forward and not too open at the base. They are set far apart and low on the head, and are well furnished with long tufts.
Eyes. Large, round, brilliant and full, wide apart, with a sweet expression.

COLOURPOINT COLOURS

All point colours are possible, as in the Siamese, though not all are recognized everywhere at the present. The more recently developed varieties include the female-only Chocolate-Tortie point and Lilac-cream point; the Smoke-points; and the Tabby-(Lynx-) points now recognized in Europe.

Coat pattern. Body should be an even pale colour, with the main contrasting colour confined to the points (mask, ears, legs and tail). The mask should cover the whole face, but not the top of the head, and be connected to the ears by tracings.

Seal-point. Body colour an even pale fawn to warm cream, shading

Above: A dilute of the Seal-point, this Blue-point Colourpoint displays a long flowing coat and deep vivid blue, round eyes. The undercoat is glacial, bluish white.

to a lighter cream on the chest and stomach. Points deep seal brown. Noseleather and paw pads seal brown. Eyes deep vivid blue. 57 ▶

Chocolate-point. Body colour ivory all over. Points warm milk-chocolate colour. Noseleather and paw pads cinnamon-pink. Eyes deep vivid blue.

Blue-point. Body colour glacial, bluish white, shading to a warmer white on the chest and stomach. Points slate blue. Noseleather and paw pads slate blue. Eyes deep vivid blue.

Lilac-point. Body colour magnolia (UK) or glacial white (USA) all over. Points frosty grey with a pinkish tone (lilac). Noseleather and paw pads lavender-pink. Eyes deep vivid blue.

Red-(Flame-) point. Body colour creamy white. Points delicate orange to red. Noseleather and paw pads flesh or coral pink. Eyes deep vivid blue.

Cream-point. Body colour creamy white. Points buff cream. Noseleather and paw pads flesh or coral pink. Eyes deep vivid blue.

Tortie-point. Body colour and basic point colour as appropriate to Seal- and Chocolate-point. Points patched with red and/or cream. A blaze of red or cream on the face is desirable. Noseleather and paw pads in keeping with the basic point colour and/or pink. Eyes deep vivid blue. 57 ▸

Blue-cream point. Body colour bluish white or creamy white, shading to white on the chest and stomach. Points blue with patches of cream. Noseleather and paw pads slate blue and/or pink. Eyes deep vivid blue.

Lilac-cream point. Body colour magnolia (UK) or glacial white (US) all over. Points frosty pinkish grey, patched with pale cream. A facial blaze is desirable. Noseleather and paw pads lavender-pink and/or pink. Eyes deep vivid blue.

Tabby-(Lynx-) point. Body colour as appropriate to the point colour, which can be seal, chocolate, blue, lilac or red. Points should carry characteristic 'M' marking on forehead, bars on face and fainter rings on legs and tail, in the appropriate solid colour, well defined from a paler background. Noseleather and paw pads in keeping with point colour. Eyes deep vivid blue in colour.

HIMALAYAN HYBRIDS

Outcrossing to other Persians made to improve type in colour-point breeding resulted in the appearance of other coloured longhaired kittens in the litters. In the United Kingdom some of these cats have now been granted official recognition as varieties of Persian (Chocolate Tortie and Lilac-cream; see page 28). In the United States, however, such cats are regarded as Himalayan Hybrids. They are useful for breeding Himalayans as they carry the appropriate genes, but they cannot be shown. They look just like Persians, but are usually much less expensive to buy and so would make excellent pets for people wanting a Persian-type cat, but not intending to show.

KASHMIR
(Self-coloured Himalayan)

The self-coloured chocolate and lilac cats that appeared during the Colourpoint breeding programme are classed as Self-coloured Persians in the United Kingdom, but as Solid-coloured Himalayans or Kashmirs (a separate breed) in the United States.

They first appeared in Colourpoint litters or in hybrid litters, where an outcross to a Persian had been made to improve type, and it has taken several years to achieve an even body colour throughout with the long flowing coat required by the standard. The Lilac is a dilute form of the Chocolate.

The show standard is the same as Colourpoint (Himalayan).

SHOW SUMMARY
Chocolate. Coat colour medium to dark chocolate brown all over, with the same depth of colour from the root to the tip of each hair and no sign of a paler undercoat. Noseleather and paw pads brown. Eyes deep orange or copper.

Lilac. Coat colour pinkish dove grey all over with no sign of a paler undercoat. Noseleather pink. Paw pads very pale pink. Eyes pale orange. 57 ▸

BALINESE (Longhaired Siamese)

Good points
- *Quieter than Siamese, vocally*
- *Lively*
- *Affectionate*
- *Good with children*
- *Very beautiful*
- *Extremely graceful*

Take heed
- *Dislikes being left alone*
- *Needs daily grooming*

A Balinese makes an excellent pet: it wants to enjoy fun and games with the family and loves people. In fact a longhaired Siamese, it resembles the Siamese in its graceful beauty, but is quieter in voice and temperament and less boisterous. It is easy to care for.

Although still rather a rare breed, the Balinese is becoming increasingly popular because of its delightful personality. A Balinese would be a good choice of pet for the person who likes the Siamese look, but prefers a less overwhelming personality!

Grooming
The Balinese is easy to groom. Although the coat is fairly long, it is very silky and non-matting. It does need daily grooming, however, to remove dead hairs and to keep the coat in good condition, but this is not the chore that it may be with a Persian. A few minutes' gentle brushing with a soft brush is all that is required.

Origin and history
The Balinese is a natural mutation derived from Siamese parents with a mutant gene for long hair. A few longhaired kittens first appeared in Siamese litters in the United States. They were soon recognized by breeders as potentially beautiful cats, and selectively bred together. First recognized as a breed in 1963, by 1970 the Balinese was recognized by all governing bodies in the United States. They have reached Europe only recently.

The name is unconnected with their origin: they were so named

Above: A Blue-point Balinese. Any Siamese colouring may occur.

because of their graceful agility, their movements resembling those of Balinese dancers.

Breeding
Longhaired Siamese kittens appear from time to time in Siamese litters. When two are mated together they breed true, producing all-Balinese kittens. Outcrossing to Siamese is necessary occasionally to improve type. Balinese litters normally contain five or six kittens.

Kittens
The kittens are born white, the point markings gradually appearing over the first few weeks.

SHOW SUMMARY
The Balinese is a medium-sized svelte and dainty cat, yet lithe and muscular, with long, tapering Siamese lines and a long silky coat.
Coat. Ermine-like, soft, silky and flowing, 5cm (2in) or more in length (although it may be shorter in summer). No downy undercoat and no ruff around the neck.

Body. Medium sized, long and svelte. Fine boned but well muscled. Males may be larger than females. Legs long and slim, hindlegs longer than forelegs. Feet dainty, small and oval.

Tail. Long, thin and tapering to a point, but well plumed.

Head. Long, tapering wedge, making a straight-edged triangle from the jaw to the ears. There should be no whisker break. The nose is long and straight with no nose break. Neck long and slender. Ears wide at the base, large and pointed. Not less than the width of an eye between the eyes.

Eyes. Medium sized, almond shaped and slanted towards the nose. No squints allowed.

BALINESE COLOURS

In the United Kingdom all colours recognized in the Siamese are now being bred. In the United States only Seal, Chocolate, Blue and Lilac are recognized for competition as Balinese; cats with other Siamese colours are known as **Javanese** but carry the same standard for type as the Balinese.

Coat pattern. Body should be an even pale colour with the main contrasting colour confined to the points (mask, ears, legs and tail). The mask should cover the whole face, but not the top of the head, and be connected to the ears by tracings. Older cats may have darker body colour.

Seal-point. Body colour an even pale fawn to warm cream, shading to a lighter cream on the chest and stomach. Points deep seal brown. Noseleather and paw pads seal brown. Eyes deep vivid blue.

Chocolate-point. Body colour ivory all over. Points warm milk-chocolate colour. Noseleather and paw pads cinnamon-pink. Eyes deep vivid blue.

Blue-point. Body colour glacial, bluish white, shading to a warmer white on the chest and stomach.

Points slate blue. Noseleather and paw pads slate blue. Eyes deep vivid blue. 58 ▶

Lilac-point. Body colour magnolia (UK) or glacial white (US) all over. Points frosty grey with a pinkish tone (lilac). Noseleather and paw pads lavender-pink. Eyes deep vivid blue.

Red-point. Body colour creamy white. Points delicate orange to red. Noseleather and paw pads flesh or coral pink. Eyes deep vivid blue.

Cream-point. Body colour creamy white. Points buff cream. Noseleather and paw pads flesh or coral pink. Eyes deep vivid blue.

Tortie-point. Body colour and basic point colour as appropriate to Seal- and Chocolate-point. Points patched with red and/or cream. A blaze of red or cream is desirable. Noseleather and paw pads in keeping with the basic point colour and/or pink. Eyes deep vivid blue.

Blue-cream point. Body colour bluish white or creamy white, shading to white on the chest and stomach. Points blue with patches of cream. Noseleather and paw pads slate blue and/or pink. Eyes deep vivid blue.

Lilac-cream point. Body colour magnolia (UK) or glacial white (US) all over. Points frosty pinkish grey, intermingled (UK) or patched (US) with pale cream. A facial blaze is desirable. Noseleather and paw pads lavender-pink and/or pink. Eyes deep vivid blue.

Tabby-(Lynx-)point. Body colour as appropriate to the point colour, which can be seal, chocolate, blue, lilac or red. Points should carry characteristic 'M' marking on forehead, bars on face and fainter rings on legs and tail, in appropriate solid colour, well defined from a paler background. Noseleather and paw pads in keeping with point colour. Eyes deep vivid blue.

BIRMAN (Sacred Cat of Burma)

Good points
- *Charming*
- *Intelligent*
- *Adaptable and easy to train*
- *Good with children*
- *Quiet*
- *Strikingly beautiful*

Take heed
- *Needs daily grooming*
- *Does not like to be caged*

Birman cats are as individual in their personalities as in their looks and have a quiet, gentle charm. Intelligent and companionable, a Birman will enjoy being part of the family and mixes well with other animals. It is adaptable and playful.

However, a Birman likes freedom to roam about the house and garden, and as it is not as prone to climb as the longer legged cats, is easier to confine to your property.

Grooming

Although the Birman's coat is said never to mat, it must be brushed and combed daily to remove dead hairs, so that these are not swallowed in large quantities and a fur ball formed in the stomach. For a show cat, a little grooming powder dusted into the paler areas of the coat will remove any grease marks.

Origin and history

The Birman, or Sacred Cat of Burma, is said to have originated in the temples of Burma. If it did, it was probably developed by natural crosses between Siamese and bicoloured longhaired cats. In France it was established in the 1920s and first recognized there in 1925. At about the same time another line was established in Germany. In 1959 the first Birmans arrived in the United States; in 1965 British breeders began to establish the breed in the UK.

Breeding

Birmans breed true to type, and

litters usually contain four kittens.

Kittens
Birman kittens are large and healthy, and seem to maintain their playful behaviour long into adulthood.

SHOW SUMMARY
The Birman is a large, longhaired cat with the Himalayan coat pattern, but with four white paws.
Coat. Long and silky with a tendency to wave on the stomach. Non-matting. Thick and heavy ruff around the neck.
Body. Medium long, but stocky and low on the legs. Legs heavy, medium in length; paws round, firm and very large with toes close together.
Tail. Medium in length and bushy. No kinks allowed.
Head. Strong, broad and rounded. Cheeks full. Roman nose with low nostrils. Ears wide apart, as wide at the base as tall, and rounded at the tips.
Eyes. Almost round.

BIRMAN COLOURS
Only four colours occur naturally within the breed: Seal-point, Chocolate-point, Blue-point and Lilac-point.

All have the characteristic white feet or 'gloves'.

Coat pattern. Body should be an even pale colour with the main contrasting colour confined to the points (mask, ears, legs and tail). The mask should cover the whole face, including the whisker pads, and is connected to the ears by tracings. The white foot markings should be symmetrical. Front paws have white gloves ending in an even line across the paw over the knuckles; in the hind paws the white glove covers the whole paw and extends up the backs of the legs to a point just below the hocks known as the 'laces' or 'gauntlets'.

Seal-point. Body colour an even pale beige to cream, warm in tone with a characteristic golden glow over the back, especially obvious in adult males. Underparts and chest are slightly paler. Points (except gloves) dark seal brown. Gloves pure white. Noseleather deep seal brown. Paw pads pink. Eyes deep violet blue. 58 ▶

Chocolate-point. Body colour even ivory all over. Points (except gloves) warm milk-chocolate colour; gloves pure white. Noseleather cinnamon-pink. Paw pads pink. Eyes deep violet blue.

Blue-point. Body colour bluish-white, cold in tone, becoming less cold on the stomach and chest. Points (except gloves) deep blue; gloves pure white. noseleather slate grey. Paw pads pink. Eyes deep violet blue.

Lilac-point. Body colour cold glacial white. points (except gloves) frosty grey-pink; gloves pure white. Noseleather lavender-pink. Paw pads pink. Eyes deep violet blue.

Left: A magnificent Seal-point Birman, which is a longhair with Himalayan coat pattern and pure white gloves on all four feet. Birmans are quiet, charming pets but they do need daily grooming.

NORWEGIAN FOREST CAT (Norsk Skogkatt)

Good points
- *Beautiful*
- *Athletic*
- *Waterproof coat*
- *Good hunter*

Take heed
- *Needs daily grooming*
- *Prefers an outdoor life*
- *Moults heavily in spring and summer*

The Norwegian Forest Cat is an outdoor-loving, active cat with a robust, hardy disposition. An amusing cat, it loves to climb high trees and comes down spirally head first! It has a unique waterproof coat that dries in about 15 minutes after heavy rain. It loves to show off in front of an audience and is affectionate, intelligent and extremely playful.

The Norwegian Forest Cat is used to a rough life and makes a good mouser. This cat would be happiest given an outdoor life where it is free to roam; confined in an apartment it might soon become bored.

Grooming
The Norwegian Forest Cat has a double coat: an undercoat that is tight and woolly, and a water-resistant silky top coat. The coat does not mat, but it needs careful daily grooming if the cat is destined for showing. To prevent fur ball, even the non-show cat should be groomed daily with a brush and comb, especially during the early summer months when the undercoat is being shed. After this, less attention is necessary until the full coat is grown again in the autumn.

Origin and history
Despite its name, which suggests a wild origin, the Norwegian Forest Cat has always been more or less domesticated in Norway, and has lived with or near man for several centuries. Even today cats of this type are frequently kept on farms.

The breed is believed to have arisen as a result of the harsh Scandinavian climate. It is likely that the cat's ancestors were both shorthaired cats from Southern Europe and longhaired cats from Asia Minor, brought into Scandinavia with traders and travellers. As domestic cats were usually kept as mousers and not as pets, they led an outdoor life; and the harsh climate may have meant that only cats with heavier coats would survive the winters.

In recent years, pedigree breeding lines of Norwegian Forest Cats have been established, and today there are about 500 registered. The breed was dignified with recognition by FIFE (Fédération Internationale Féline d'Europe) in 1977 and is now accepted for competition at all European shows. At present, however, the breed is little known outside Europe, and most cats are bred in Norway.

Breeding
Naturally robust, the queens kitten easily and make attentive mothers.

Kittens
Norwegian forest kittens are healthy and playful. The first adult coat begins to grow at three to five months of age.

SHOW SUMMARY
The Norwegian Forest Cat should give the impression of strength, being well built and muscular, with a long body and long legs. The characteristic feature is the shaggy weather-resistant coat.

Coat. Very long top coat; guard hairs are smooth and oily, making the coat water-repellent. Tight woolly undercoat. In autumn a ruff grows around the neck and chest, but this is shed the following summer. Coat quality may vary with living conditions: cats kept indoors for much of the time have softer, shorter coats.

Body. Long, large and heavily built. Legs long; hind legs longer than forelegs. Feet wide, with heavy paws. Slender type is a fault.

Tail. Long and well furnished.

Head. Triangular in shape, with a long, wide, straight nose without a nose break. Neck long. Cheeks full. Chin heavy. Ears long, set high on the head, upright and pointed, well furnished inside with long ear tufts. Whiskers prominent and long. Faults include a short nose, small or wide-set ears.

Eyes. Large, open and set wide apart.

NORWEGIAN FOREST CAT COLOURS

Any coat colour or pattern is permitted, with or without white. Commonly white appears on the chest and paws. Tabby cats generally have heavier coats than the solid and bicoloured varieties. Eye colour should be in keeping with the coat colour. 59 ▶

Below: A fine looking Norwegian Forest Cat with thick tabby coat.

MAINE COON

Good points
- *Hardy and active*
- *Fun-loving*
- *Quiet, unique voice*
- *Good with children*
- *Even-tempered*
- *Easy to care for*
- *Good mouser*

Take heed
- *No drawbacks known*

The Maine Coon is a large cat, very hardy and active, and good with children, but shy. It is good-tempered, easy to groom and to care for. It loves playing and performing tricks, and has a delightful quiet, chirping voice; no two Maine Coons will sound alike. Distinctive in appearance, the cat is almost shorthaired in front and longhaired along the back and stomach. Used to harsh climates and to living rough, the Maine Coon is apt to sleep in strange positions and in peculiar places. Although adaptable to indoor or outdoor life, this cat would prefer plenty of space to roam.

Requiring little grooming, it makes an ideal pet for the person who likes the beauty of a long-haired cat, but does not have the time to devote to daily grooming.

Grooming
The Maine Coon's undercoat is slight, so the cat is easy to groom and a gentle brushing and combing every few days will suffice to remove dead hairs.

Origin and history
Like many breeds of cat, the Maine Coon's origin is largely unknown. Most likely, it developed from matings between domestic shorthaired cats and longhaired cats brought by traders from Asia Minor to Maine and other parts of New England, long before records of cats were kept.

It is possible that in its early days, the Maine Coon may have roamed free, and was given the name 'coon cat' because of its similarity in

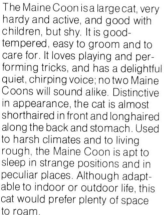

appearance and habits to the native raccoon. Both have long fur, climb trees and, as tabby is the common pattern among non-pedigree cats, have fur of a similar colour and ringed tails.

Although no early records were kept, the Maine Coon was well known in the East Coast states by the end of the nineteenth century. They were kept as mousers long before they became show cats, but were one of the earliest breeds seen at cat shows: many Maine Coons were exhibited at the first New York cat show in 1860, and a Maine Coon was Best Cat in Show at a Madison Square Garden show in New York in 1895. After that time, however, interest in the breed almost died out until the formation of the Maine Coon Cat Club in 1953 revived interest, and held regular one-breed shows for them.

The Maine Coon is no longer confined to the state from which it takes its name, but is well known and bred throughout the United States, and now even in Europe.

Breeding
Maine Coons usually have only one litter per year and make good mothers. Because of the breed's mixed background, the litters often contain a colourful assortment of kittens.

Kittens
The large, robust kittens mature slowly and may take up to four years to develop their full beauty.

SHOW SUMMARY
The Maine coon is a tough, large

and rugged cat, solidly built, with a smooth, shaggy coat.

Coat. Heavy and shaggy, yet silky in texture, lustrous and flowing. Short on the face and shoulders, but longer on the stomach and hind legs, where it forms long, shaggy breeches.

Body. A long-bodied cat with a broad chest and level back, giving a rectangular appearance. Males 4.5-5.4kg (10-12lb); females smaller, 3.6-4.5kg (8-10lb). Muscular, with strong legs set wide apart. Feet large and round. Paws well tufted.

Tail. Blunt ended, but well furnished with long fur, and plume-like. Wider at the base. No kinks allowed.

Head. Small in proportion to the body, set on a medium length powerful neck. Square muzzle. Firm chin, not undershot. High cheekbones. Nose is medium length and may have a slight nose break. Ears large and well tufted, wide at the base and tapering to a point; set high on the head.

Eyes. Slightly slanting, large and set wide apart.

MAINE COON COLOURS

Maine Coons are bred in all coat colours and patterns, and combinations of colours and patterns, such as tabby with white. In this case, there should be white on the bib, stomach and all four paws, and preferably on one-third of the body. Eye colour can be green, gold or copper, though white cats may also be blue-eyed or odd-eyed. There is no relationship between eye colour and coat colour or pattern.

The colour standards for show cats are the same as those given for Persians. 59 ▶

Below: A typical Brown Tabby-and-white Maine Coon. These large cats come in all coat colours and patterns.

ANGORA (Turkish Angora)

Good points
- *Very beautiful*
- *Graceful*
- *Intelligent*
- *Loyal*
- *Friendly*
- *Quiet*

Take heed
- *Needs some daily grooming*
- *Moults in spring and summer*

The Angora makes a charming, dainty companion and is very attractive in appearance, with its long lithe body and plumed tail. It is not a talkative cat but is loyal, affectionate and adaptable; it would be happy living in either town or country, but would prefer to be given the run of the home. Alert, lively and intelligent, it loves to play games and to show off to an audience.

Angoras are bred in most colours and patterns, although white is probably the most popular. Some of the blue-eyed and odd-eyed whites may be deaf, and it is advisable to make sure before purchase that your chosen kitten is not deaf, unless you feel competent to take full care of such an animal and protect it against the inevitable dangers.

At present the Angora is still a rather rare breed, and may be expensive to buy. However, it is possible to purchase a non-show class kitten more reasonably.

Grooming
Although the Angora is easier to groom than a Persian, it nevertheless needs and will enjoy a daily grooming session. Use a medium-toothed comb with a handle to remove dead hairs. Grooming is particularly important in spring and early summer when much of the coat is shed.

Origin and history
The Angora is thought to be the oldest longhaired breed in Europe and came originally from Ankara in Turkey, where it is known to exist today, both as a free roaming domestic cat and in the local zoo.

Angoras arrived in the United Kingdom via France at the end of the sixteenth century, and so were known for a time as French cats. In the early days they were unfortunately mated indiscriminately with other longhaired cats (the original Persians), and in the process the Persian type was dominant and the Angora type was lost until quite recently, except of course in Turkey. Apparently the early Persians had long, thick coats, lacking the silkiness of the Angora coat, and it is thought that Angoras may have been used to improve the Persian coat.

Recently the breed has been revived in the Eastern United States, where cats have been imported direct from the Ankara Zoo. These cats are white, but other colours have been bred and many are now recognized for showing on both sides of the Atlantic, although numbers in the United Kingdom are still small.

Breeding
Angora litters usually contain four to five kittens, though six or seven is not uncommon. Although many colours occur naturally within the breed, white is so dominant that it nearly always appears in the coat, and it is difficult to produce show quality Angoras in other colours.

Deafness is particularly common among blue-eyed and odd-eyed white Angoras, and unless you are prepared to take on considerable responsibility, it is best not to use a deaf cat for breeding.

Above: Chocolate is a popular colour within the Angora breed and amber eyes are preferred. A lovely foreign-type cat with long hair, giving a graceful effect.

Kittens
Angora kittens are charming, fluffy and playful. White kittens born with a smudge of black hairs on the top of their heads are likely to have good hearing in at least one ear. The kittens mature slowly, and the long, silky coat is not fully developed until two years of age.

SHOW SUMMARY
The Angora is a medium-sized cat, solidly built, but graceful and lithe, with a long, flowing coat.
Coat. Medium length silky hair; slightly wavy, especially on the stomach. No thick woolly under-coat. The hair is long on the under-parts and ruff, and shorter along the back and on the face.
Body. Medium in size, long, graceful and lithe. Fine but strong-boned. Long but sturdy legs; hind legs slightly longer than forelegs. Feet small, oval to round and dainty; toes well tufted.
Tail. Long and tapering, wider at the base and well plumed. When moving, the tail is carried horizontally over the body, sometimes almost touching the head.
Head. Medium sized, wide, gently pointed wedge. Nose straight without a stop. Neck long and slim. Ears set high on head, large and pointed, broad based and tufted.
Eyes. Large, round to oval in shape and slightly slanted.

ANGORA COLOURS
Chalky white is the favourite colour, but all other longhaired coat colours are accepted. Particularly liked are Black, Blue, Chocolate and Lilac in self and tabby patterns, Red, Tortoiseshell, Cinnamon and Bicolours. (Chocolate and Lilac are not accepted in the United States.) Eyes are amber in all colours, but Brown and Silver Tabbies may have green or hazel eyes, and Whites may be blue- or odd-eyed (one blue, one amber). Balinese have the same body shape as Angoras. 60 ▶

Black Persian 12 ▶

White Persian 10 ▶

Left: Some people may think that odd eyes are a little strange but this is one of the recognized eye colours at cat shows for White Persians. Blue-eyed Whites may be deaf from birth and some Odd-eyed Whites are deaf on the blue-eyed side. White Persians are really beautiful cats but they need daily grooming to keep their coats free from hard knots. Talcum powder or chalk-based grooming powder may be brushed into the cat's coat to keep it white.

Blue Persian 13 ▶

Black-and-white
Bicolour Persian 16 ▶

Cream Persian
kitten 15 ▶

Red Persian 14 ▶

Right: A Bicolour is not just
a two-coloured cat. The
colours must be white with
one other colour, but with
proportions laid down for
the show standard by the
Governing Bodies in each
country. The pattern should
be symmetrical with patches
of colour on the head and
body. This Blue-and-white
Persian Bicolour shows the
facial blaze of white which
is a preferred feature of
the breed. Tabby markings
and white hairs in the
colour patches are faults.

Cameo Tabby Persian 16 ▶

Shell Cameo Persian 16 ▶

Chinchilla Persian 16 ▶

Shaded Cameo Persian 22 ▶

Shaded Silver Persian 22 ▶

Blue Smoke
Persian 23 ▶

Left: Cats with coats that are very lightly tipped with a contrasting colour are known as Chinchillas. This one is a Chinchilla Golden, with cream fur tipped with seal. Chinchilla cats are very robust and healthy.

Right: Heavily tipped cats are called Smokes. Some even look solid-coloured until they move and show the undercoat. This Black Smoke has a white undercoat, silver ruff and black face and feet.

*Tortoiseshell-and-white
(Calico) Persian* 27 ▶

*Tortoiseshell
Persian* 25 ▶

Blue-cream Persian (UK) 26 ▶

Brown Classic
(Blotched) Tabby Persian 29 ▶

Silver Classic
Tabby Persian 29 ▶

Red Mackerel
Tabby Persian 29 ▶

Left: A lovely Blue Tortoiseshell-and-white (Dilute
Calico) Persian with deep
copper coloured eyes. This
is one of latest of the
particolours and is a joy to
behold. These cats make
sweet companions.

Right: This beautiful Seal
Tabby-point Colourpoint was
developed by crossing the
Brown Tabby Persian with a
Seal-point Colourpoint. Cats
with this very attractive
Himalayan coat pattern all
have blue eyes.

Chocolate-point
Bicolour Ragdoll 34 ▶

Lilac-point Bicolour
Ragdoll kitten 34 ▶

Red Tabby
Peke-faced Persian 32 ▶

Lilac Kashmir 39 ▶

*Tortie-point
Colourpoint* 36 ▶

*Seal-point
Colourpoint* 36 ▶

Left: *Two Seal-point Colour-point Ragdoll kittens and one Mitted Seal-point Ragdoll kitten. Like all Himalayan-patterned cats, these three were born white, the points and coat shading developing gradually. They make gentle pets but are rare in Europe.*

Right: *During the develop-ment of Colourpoints it was inevitable that some solid-coloured cats would appear like this Chocolate Kashmir kitten. Lilac is the other colour known for Kashmirs.*

Blue-point Balinese 40 ▶

Seal-point Birman 42 ▶

Left: This lovely cat is a Lilac-point Balinese. A Siamese type with long hair, it has a quieter voice and less boisterous personality, characteristics which are making this delightful breed increasingly popular.

Right: Maine Coons are found mainly in the United States, and as these kittens show, they come in all colours and combinations. They are hardy and fun-loving, and make ideal pets being easy to care for and good with children.

Brown Tabby-and-white
Norwegian Forest Cat 44 ▶

Blue-and-white
Bicolour Maine Coon 46 ▶

Amber-eyed White Angora 48 ▶

Turkish 64 ▶

Turkish kitten 64 ▶

Blue Tortoiseshell-and-white (Dilute Calico) Cymric 66 ▶

Sorrel (Red) Somali kitten 68 ▶

Ruddy Somali 68 ▶

Left: Although white is probably the most popular colour for an Angora, many other colours and patterns occur. Here a Blue-cream mother has produced Black, White and Cream kittens. The lovely coat does not develop fully until two years old.

Right: Somalis are longhaired Abyssinians and may occur in the same colours. This is a Ruddy or Normal kitten. Like Angoras, it may take up to two years for the silky coat to develop fully.

Odd-eyed White
British Shorthair 72 ▶

Black British
Shorthair 71 ▶

Left: British Shorthairs are the native cats of the UK and come in all the usual colours. They are especially healthy cats because they are a natural breed rather than one created by breeders. Seen here is the Orange-eyed form of the much prized White British Shorthair. Pure white cats such as this have always been rather rare, but if destined for a show career the coat must have no yellow tinge or grey areas. All British Shorthairs make attractive pets.

Red-and-white
Bicolour British
Shorthair 75 ▶

Blue British
Shorthair 73 ▶

Tipped British
Shorthair (Chinchilla) 75 ▶

Cream British Shorthair 74 ▶

Right: This cat is a pretty
Cream Tipped Shorthair, with
orange eyes. British Tipped
Shorthairs have white undercoats and tipping of any British
Shorthair colour, with the
addition of lilac and
chocolate. They are some
of the newest cats to appear
on the show bench. The
kittens tend to have longer
coats at birth than is
normal for British Short-
hairs because of the longhaired cats in their
ancestry, but this is lost
when the adult coat grows.

TURKISH (Turkish Van cat)

Good points
- *Distinctive appearance*
- *Elegant*
- *Intelligent*
- *Hardy*
- *Likes playing with water and can swim*

Take heed
- *Needs some daily grooming*
- *Moults in spring and summer*

The Turkish cat makes an exotically different pet, with its beautiful chalk-white coat and striking auburn face and tail. Its main claim to originality is that it enjoys swimming and playing with water. In colder climates, care must be taken to ensure that the cat does not catch cold, although in its native Turkey the winters are very severe, and Turkish cats are generally strong and hardy.

This is still a rare breed, so you must expect to pay quite a lot and

Below: Turkish are fun as they like water and swimming but must not catch cold. Intelligent and really affectionate, they make good pets.

to have to wait for a kitten, as demand will probably exceed the supply. It is worth the wait, however, as the Turkish cat is lively and affectionate and makes a charming, intelligent companion. A neutered male would make an excellent pet and may be obtained more reasonably because not as many studs will be kept for breeding as female kittens.

Grooming
The Turkish is an easy cat to groom, but a light daily combing is recommended to remove dead hairs, particularly when the cat is moulting in spring and summer. Occasionally a little non-toxic

grooming powder may be dusted into the coat to keep away greasy marks, which would otherwise mar the lovely chalk-white appearance. Unlike many other cats, the Turkish will enjoy a bath, but keep the animal warm afterwards to prevent it catching a chill.

Origin and history
Turkish cats are thought to have originated as a result of natural selection due to interbreeding within a geographically isolated area, the Van region of Turkey, where they have been domesticated for centuries. They were first introduced into the United Kingdom in the 1950s, when a pair was brought from Turkey by an English breeder. The line was gradually established, with more cats being imported from Turkey, and is now becoming popular in Europe.

At present the breed is not recognized for competition in the United States, although some are bred and kept as pets.

Breeding
Turkish cats breed true, the kittens always resembling their parents, and the breed is being kept pure by not outcrossing to any other breed or colour variety. The average litter contains four kittens.

Below: A Turkish Cat with chalk white fur, auburn markings, round amber eyes and pink noseleather.

Kittens
The kittens are born pure chalk white — not pink, like most all-white animals — with the auburn markings already quite clearly visible. Their eyes open very early, at four or five days, and are blue, gradually changing to pale amber.

SHOW SUMMARY
The Turkish is a medium-sized cat, sturdy and strong in build, with a long, silky coat. Males are rather larger and more muscular than females.
Coat. Very silky, long, straight fur, without a thick woolly undercoat.
Body. Long but sturdy, with medium-length legs. Feet small and round, with tufted toes.
Tail. Medium in length and full.
Head. Short and wedge-shaped. Medium-length neck. Nose long, not snub. Ears large, upright, close together, shell pink inside and well tufted.
Eyes. Round, pink-rimmed.

TURKISH COLOUR
Chalk white with auburn markings on the face, around and below the ears, with a white blaze continuing up between the ears. Nose, cheeks and chin are white. The tail is ringed in two shades of auburn, and the tail markings are particularly obvious in kittens. Small auburn markings are allowed elsewhere on the body. Noseleather and paw pads pale pink. Eyes pale amber. 60 ▶

CYMRIC (Longhaired Manx)

Good points
- *Intelligent*
- *Quiet*
- *Affectionate*
- *Strong*
- *Gentle*
- *Good mouser*
- *Good with children and dogs*

Take heed
- *Needs daily grooming*

The Cymric's unique appearance distinguishes it from other cats: it has no tail, but it differs from the Manx in that it also has long hair. The Cymric has the same temperament and personality as the Manx, being loyal and affectionate, intelligent and gentle, courageous and strong. It makes an excellent family pet, being good with children and dogs, and is amusing as well as sensitive. Like the Manx it would make an excellent mouser for offices or hotels, especially since there is no tail to get caught in doors! A fast runner and a good hunter, the Cymric needs plenty of space to roam.

Grooming
Although the Cymric has long hair, the fur does not mat easily, and the cat is therefore easy to groom. A good comb-through daily is all that is required to remove dead hairs. Their eyes and ears should be examined regularly for dirt or ear mites.

Origin and history
The Manx is an old-established breed, particularly common on the Isle of Man, but also known elsewhere. However, it seems that longhaired kittens first appeared in Manx litters in Canada in the 1960s. At no time in recorded pedigree cat breeding history was the Manx knowingly outcrossed to a longhaired cat, but it is reasonable to assume that a recessive gene for long hair must have been present for many generations. Consequently, the Cymric is one of the newer breeds in the show ring, and

is confined at present to North America.

Breeding
Mating two Cymrics produces 100 percent Cymric kittens, but tail-less cats have a lethal factor when like is mated to like too often; therefore for the best results tailed or stumpy tailed cats should be mated to tail-less cats. The show animal must, however, be completely tail-less, with a hollow where the root of the tail should be. Many of the tailed or stumpy tailed kittens that are born in the same litters make excellent pets, and are just as intelligent and affectionate.

Kittens
Cymric kittens are courageous and venturesome and very playful, even though denied the built-in toy that other breeds have in the nest, that inviting feature — mother's tail.

SHOW SUMMARY
The principal feature in the show Cymric is a complete absence of tail. The whole cat should have a round, rabbity look, with a short back and long hind legs.
Coat. Medium to long and double. The undercoat is thick and cottony. The top coat is silky and glossy.
Body. A solid, rounded cat, with a short back, rounded rump, very deep flanks and muscular thighs. The forelegs are set well apart and are short and heavily boned. The hind legs are longer than the forelegs. The back is arched from the shoulder to the rump. The feet are neat and round.
Tail. Absent, with a decided hollow

at the end of the spine. A residual tail is a fault.

Head. Large and round, with prominent cheekbones. Short, thick neck, and strong chin. Nose of medium length with a gentle nose break. The whisker pads are rounded and there is a decided whisker break. Ears are large, wide at the base, tapering to slightly pointed tips, set on top of the head, and with ear tufts at the ends.

Eyes. Large, round and expressive; set at an angle to the nose, outer corners being slightly higher than inner corners.

CYMRIC COLOURS
All coat colours and patterns and combinations of coat colours and patterns, such as white with tabby, are permitted. However, Chocolate, Lilac and the Himalayan pattern are not accepted, nor these colours with white. For colour standards, see Persians. 61 ▶

Below: A Cymric or Longhair Manx with tabby coat, looking strong and healthy. This pretty cat makes the perfect family pet as it is good with children and it will act as a really effective rodent officer!

SOMALI

Good points
- *Easy to groom*
- *Almost voiceless*
- *Amusing and entertaining*
- *Affectionate*
- *Even-tempered*
- *Good with children*
- *Easy to care for*

Take heed
- *Does not like to be caged*

The Somali is a longhaired Abyssinian, similar in temperament and colouring, but a little less boisterous. The Somali makes an interesting pet, as it is playful and lively, yet very quiet to have around, being almost voiceless. Gentle and well-mannered, it makes an excellent family pet, and is almost always good tempered.

However, like the Abyssinian, a Somali would be happiest if given plenty of freedom and space to run around; it may fret if caged.

Grooming
Although fairly long, the Somali coat does not mat and therefore daily grooming is not essential, though a run-through with a medium-toothed comb is advisable to remove dead hairs, and will probably be appreciated by the cat.

Origin and history
Longhaired kittens began to appear in Abyssinian litters in Canada and the United States, and even in Europe, during the 1960s, and were thought to be a natural mutation. However, most of their ancestry can be traced back to Abyssinians in the United Kingdom that were experimentally mated to longhaired cats. Consequently, it is now thought that the gene for long hair was introduced by breeders. The subsequent export of British- and American-bred Abyssinians all over the world has spread the longhaired factor abroad, and so attractive is it that some Abyssinian breeders in Australia are now concentrating on breeding the Somali instead of the Abyssinian.

The first breed club was formed in 1972, and by 1978 the breed was officially recognized by all the various American and Canadian governing bodies.

Breeding
Mating two Somalis will produce all-Somali kittens, but they may also appear in Abyssinian litters where both parents carry the gene for long hair. Somalis can also be mated to Abyssinians to improve type.

Kittens
Somali litters rarely contain more than three or four kittens and the ratio of males to females is high. They are slightly larger than Abyssinian kittens, and are slower to develop their full adult coats.

SHOW SUMMARY
The Somali is a medium-sized, lithe-bodied cat, firm and muscular, with a long coat and distinctive colouring.
Coat. Full, dense, silky and fine-textured. A ruff around the neck and breeches are desirable. The coat is longer on the stomach and shorter over the shoulders. The full beauty of the coat may take as long as two years from birth to develop.
Body. Medium in length, lithe, graceful and muscular. Rib cage rounded. Back slightly arched. Legs long and slim. Paws small and oval, with tufted toes.
Tail. Full brush; thick at the base and gently tapering.
Head. Rounded short wedge, all lines gently curving. Wide between

the ears, which are large and alert, pointed, wide at the base, set well apart towards the back of the head, and furnished with long ear tufts. Chin rounded, firm and full. No whisker break. Slight nose break.
Eyes. Almond-shaped, large, brilliant and expressive.

SOMALI COLOURS

At present the Somali is recognized in two colours — Ruddy and Sorrel (Red) — although, with Abyssinians being bred in different colours, more colours are likely to appear in due course.

Ruddy. Coat colour orange-brown, each hair ticked (banded) with black. The first band should start next to the skin, and double or treble banding is preferred. On the back there is darker shading that forms a line along the spine and continues along the tail, which ends in a black tip. The ears should be tipped with black or dark brown. The face is characteristically marked with a short, dark vertical line above each eye, and another line continues from the upper eyelid towards the ear. The eyes

Above: The Sorrel (Red) Somali is a quiet, even-tempered pet, affectionate and much admired.

are dark-rimmed and surrounded by a pale area. The underside, insides of the legs and chest should be an even ruddy colour, without ticking or other markings. The toe tufts on all four feet are black or dark brown, with black between the toes extending up the back of the hind legs. White or off-white is allowed only on the upper throat, lips and nostrils. Noseleather brick red. Paw pads black or brown. Eyes gold or green, deeper colours preferred. 61 ▶

Sorrel (Red). Body colour warm red ticked with chocolate brown. Deeper shades of red preferred. The ears and tail should be tipped with chocolate brown. The underside, insides of the legs and chest are reddish brown without ticking or other markings. The toe tufts are chocolate brown, the colour extending slightly beyond the paws. Noseleather rosy pink. Paw pads pink. Eyes gold or green, deeper colours preferred. 61 ▶

BRITISH SHORTHAIR

Good points
- *Strong and sturdy*
- *Healthy*
- *Good mouser*
- *Affectionate*
- *Good with children and dogs*
- *Quiet*
- *Easy to groom*

Take heed
- *No drawbacks known*

Because the British Shorthair is a natural breed that has not been altered to suit a breeder's whims, it is healthy and sound in mind and body. Not susceptible to illnesses and even-tempered, it will make an excellent pet for children and old people. The most popular colour is probably the Blue, followed by the Silver Tabby and the spotted varieties. Basically, this is a strong, sturdy shorthaired cat; it is active, graceful, intelligent and curious.

British Shorthairs are less expensive than most other breeds. It may be possible to obtain, for nothing, a cat that resembles this breed, but one is never sure that the kitten comes from sturdy, reliable stock. With a pedigree kitten from a reliable breeder, it should be possible to have a healthy, trouble-free pet that could be with the family for 20 years, barring accidents.

Grooming
Daily grooming is advisable to remove dead hairs, together with lots of hand stroking, which the cat will love. However, a weekly combing is sufficient to keep a British Shorthair looking neat and trim, and therefore anyone who leads a very busy life would find a shorthaired cat to be the best choice.

Origin and history
Records of pedigree cats have been kept for less than 100 years, but it is well known from history books, literature of the day and art forms that these cats have been around for centuries. They were some of the first to be shown at the end of the nineteenth century, when shows first started in the United Kingdom, and they are generally regarded as being native to the British Isles, although some of the strains may have been imported by the Romans. All the earliest known cats were shorthaired, even on the show bench. Longhaired cats have been known in Europe only since the sixteenth century. Once cat shows started, however, the longhaired cats superseded the shorthaired cats numerically on the show bench.

British shorthaired cats were imported into North America by the early English immigrants, who took them to their new home as pets and mousers. These cats mated with other shorthaired cats brought to America from other parts of the world, and gave rise to the American Shorthair breed. Both the British and American Shorthairs are therefore breeds recognized by the American associations.

Shorthaired cats are bred in Europe and closely resemble the British Shorthair. Often breeding stock is imported from the United Kingdom and the standards set for the breed and its colour varieties are very similar to those in Britain. Only the Chartreuse in France is said to differ because of its distinct history, but in recent years, the British Blue and the Chartreuse have become almost indistinguishable.

SHOW SUMMARY
The British Shorthair is a medium

Above: A Black British Shorthair with plush coat and bright eyes.

to large cat; strong and sturdy on short legs and with a short, thick coat. Males are larger than females.

Coat. Short, resilient and dense, without being double or woolly.

Body. Hard and muscular, medium to large, with a full, broad chest built on strong, short legs and with a level back. The straight forelegs are the same length as the hindlegs. The paws are neat, well rounded and firm.

Tail. Short, thick at the base, tapering to a round tip.

Head. Broad and rounded, the face round on a short neck. The nose is straight, broad and short, without a stop. The ears are set apart so that the inner ear and eye corners are perpendicular to each other; the ears are small and rounded.

Eyes. Large, round and level. They should be wide awake and full of expression. There should be the width of an eye between the eyes.

BRITISH SHORTHAIR COLOURS

Seventeen colours are recognized in the United Kingdom, but every colour known to cats is possible and will probably appear in time.

BRITISH BLACK

Black cats have a long and chequered past. In the Middle Ages they were often persecuted for being the familiars of witches, and generally regarded with suspicion. At other times in history, as now, they were considered lucky, at least in the United Kingdom. They are certainly very striking and often have very healthy-looking, glossy coats. The current show standard calls for deep copper eyes; whereas many black non-pedigree cats have lovely coats but decidedly green eyes.

Grooming

Preparing a shorthaired Black for showing requires very little trouble, but the coat must be combed daily. A little bay rum used to clean the coat for a few days before the show is an advantage, and will enhance the shine. The coat may become bleached in strong sunlight, so black cats are best shown in the winter months.

Breeding

Black cats can be obtained by mating two Blacks, or they can appear in Tortoiseshell litters. Blacks themselves are very valuable in producing Tortoiseshells and Tortoiseshell-and-whites (Calicos) and in Bicolour breeding. Type can be improved by mating Blacks to Blues, or even to Black Persians, provided that the long-haired kittens resulting from the mating are not used again for breeding, but are neutered and sold as pets.

Kittens

Black kittens may look rusty coloured when very young, but the reddish tinge disappears as the cat approaches adulthood. The important thing to look for is a coat that is a solid black down to the roots. There should be no white hairs, and the eyes should be pure copper with no tinge of green when changing from baby blue.

SHOW SUMMARY

The dense coat should be glossy and an even jet black throughout

Below: A neat Orange-eyed White British Shorthair showing the typical head and ear set.

from root to tip, with no white hairs. Noseleather and paw pads black. Eyes brilliant copper or orange with no green tinge. 62 ▶

BRITISH WHITE

There are three types of pedigree shorthaired White cat: those with blue eyes; those with orange eyes; and those with one of each colour (odd-eyed). Non-pedigree white cats usually have green eyes.

White cats have always been loved for their pure looks and were particularly prized in Japan where they were regarded as symbols of purity and perfection. There have been white cats ever since there have been cats, but despite their obvious popularity, they have always been rather rare.

Grooming

A white cat, even if it looks after itself well, will need daily grooming to remove dead hairs, and it will need more careful attention if destined for a show career. It may be necessary to shampoo the coat a week before the show, being careful to keep the animal warm after the bath. When it is dry, baby powder can be shaken into the

coat and then brushed out again. A show White must have an immaculate coat, with no yellow tinge or grey areas. All signs of powder must be removed before show day, and the whole coat smoothed with a silk handkerchief.

Breeding
Blue-eyed White cats are often deaf, which may contribute to their rarity, as deaf cats are not used frequently for breeding. Orange-eyed Whites solved the deafness problem, but in the process of their development, Odd-eyed White cats also appeared: such animals may have perfect hearing or may be deaf on the blue-eyed side. If a deaf queen is used for breeding, she will require more supervision than a normal cat because she cannot hear the cries of her kittens. She should be placed on a hard surface covered with newspaper for warmth, so she can feel her kittens and the vibrations of cries.

The average White litter contains three or four kittens, and all the kittens are born with blue eyes. Those destined to have orange eyes begin to change colour at about two weeks. The odd eyes are readily distinguished, as there is a difference in the depth of the blue colour from the start. Whites can be mated to Whites or to solid Blacks, Reds, Creams and Blues, to produce Bicolours; or to Tortoiseshells to produce Tortoiseshell-and-whites (Calicos).

Kittens
It is said that even a single black hair in the coat of a blue-eyed kitten will mean that the cat will have good hearing, at least in one ear. White kittens of any eye colour are always sought after and seem to take a pride in their appearance.

SHOW SUMMARY
The coat colour should be pure white with no yellow tinge. Noseleather and paw pads pink. Eyes gold, orange or copper; very deep sapphire blue; or one gold or copper, one deep blue. 62 ▶

BRITISH BLUE

The British Blue, with its light blue, plush coat, is the most popular of all the British shorthaired varieties in the United Kingdom. Blues are said to prefer a quiet life and are renowned for their quiet, well-balanced temperaments.

Although shown in reasonable numbers at the first cat shows, during the Second World War there were very few studs available. After the War outcrosses to other breeds were made, which unfortunately resulted in loss of type. Further outcrosses were made to longhaired Blues that did improve type, however, although they produced coats that were too long. Selective breeding during the 1950s saw the re-establishment of the shorthaired Blues, and now kittens are much in demand.

Grooming
For Blue Shorthairs, this will entail a daily combing to remove dead hairs and lots of hand stroking, which all cats enjoy. It should not be necessary to shampoo a Blue, but a little bay rum rubbed into the coat the day before the show will remove any greasiness, which otherwise might mar the colour.

Breeding
It is advisable to outcross to longhaired Blues or shorthaired Blacks occasionally to maintain good type and colour. Some of the resulting kittens will have undesirable features such as over-long fur; these are not suitable for the show bench, but, of course, make excellent and charming pets. Litters usually contain three or four kittens. Blues are particularly useful for producing Blue-creams, when mated to Creams.

Kittens
Blue kittens are especially pretty. They are usually born with faint tabby markings, but these disappear within the first few months as the coat grows.

SHOW SUMMARY
The coat colour should be a light to medium blue, sound from root to tip with no white hairs or tabby markings. Noseleather and paw pads blue. Eyes brilliant copper or orange in colour. 63 ▸

CHARTREUSE
(Chartreux)

The Chartreuse is a shorthaired blue cat similar to the British Blue, although some maintain that it is different. The breed was said to have developed in France in the Carthusian monastery of the monks who made the liqueur Chartreuse. Apparently the monks originally brought the cats from South Africa.

Wherever it came from, the Chartreuse has a long history in France and some claim to fame. The French author Colette (1873-1954), who was a great lover of cats and kept many Persians throughout her life, nevertheless chose a Chartreuse as her last companion, and it was with her when she died. The French poet Joachim du Bellay (1522-60) is reputed to have been very fond of a blue-grey cat, which could have been a Chartreuse.

Above: A Chartreuse is virtually a British Blue Shorthair. Both have a blue coat and orange eyes.

In its early days, the Chartreuse was a larger, more massive cat with a grey-blue coat, but recently, selective breeding has brought the type much closer to the British Blue and now most governing bodies in Europe accept the same standard for both cats. (See British Blue).

BRITISH CREAM

The British Cream Shorthair is a very attractive variety, but comparatively rare. The coat should be a pale, even cream with no tabby markings, and in practice this is very difficult to achieve.

Pedigree Cream Shorthairs have never been very numerous. This is partly due to the fact that in the early days of pedigree cat breeding no one knew for sure how to produce these cats to order. They appeared from time to time in Tortoiseshell litters and were usually regarded as 'sports' or freaks. They were not recognized for competition until the late 1920s.

Grooming
Preparing a Cream Shorthair for showing may require a shampoo a few days previously, as any grease or dirt in the coat will mar the colour. It also needs daily combing to remove dead hairs, and lots of hand stroking. No hand cream!

Breeding
To breed good Cream Shorthairs is not easy because, like red, of which cream is a dilute genetically, the colour is sex-linked to produce more males than females. However, they can be produced from Tortoiseshells and from Blue-creams. The Blue-cream with Blue or Cream sires produce the best Creams, and it seems that these matings are of benefit to both Blues and Creams, making the varieties of especially good type.

Kittens
Cream female kittens are obtained by mating a Blue-cream to a

Cream sire; Cream males are obtained by mating a Blue-cream to a Blue sire. Creams are very attractive as kittens, although few possess the desired pale coat; many have tabby markings or are too dark to be shown. Nevertheless they make delightful pets and will not be difficult to find homes for.

SHOW SUMMARY
The coat should be a light even cream all over without white hairs or markings of any kind. Noseleather and paw pads pink. Eyes brilliant copper or orange. 63 ▶

BRITISH BICOLOUR SHORTHAIR

Two-coloured cats have been common for centuries and were seen at the earliest cat shows, although they did not achieve official recognition as a variety until relatively recently, when they were found to be essential in the breeding of Tortoiseshell-and-whites and dilute Calicos.

The Bicolour is particularly attractive when the standard is met, although the symmetrical distribution of the colour patches and white is, in practice, very hard to achieve. This may account for the comparative scarcity of this variety on the showbench. Bicolours may be Black-and-white (Magpie), Blue-and-white, Red-and-white or more rarely, Cream-and-white.

Grooming
Bicolours are easy to groom and just need a daily combing and hand stroking. The paler colours may require a shampoo a few days before a show. Powder should not be used on the black parts or it may detract from the colour.

Breeding
Bicoloured cats appear in mixed litters of Self-coloured and Tortoiseshell-and-white kittens and result from matings between Self-coloured males and Tortoiseshell-and-white females, between Bicolour males and Tortoiseshell-and-white females and between two Bicolours or a Self-coloured and a White cat.

Bicoloured queens make excellent mothers and have kittens of various colours, according to the sire involved and both parents' genetic backgrounds.

Kittens
Bicolour kittens are very colourful; they mature early and are independent, intelligent, healthy and hardy.

SHOW SUMMARY
The show Bicolour must have a certain percentage of white and colour on the body. The patches must be distinct from the white, never intermingled. The coat pattern should be similar to that of a Dutch rabbit, with symmetrical patches of colour (either black, blue, red or cream) evenly distributed on the head, body and tail, with white predominantly on the feet, legs, face, chest and underparts. Not more than two-thirds should be coloured, and not more than a half should be white. A white facial blaze is desirable, and the markings should be as symmetrical as possible on both sides of the body. Tabby markings and white hairs in the colour patches are faults. Noseleather and paw pads according to the 'main' colour or pink. Eyes brilliant copper or orange. 63 ▶

BRITISH TIPPED SHORTHAIR

These cats are the shorthaired equivalents of the longhaired Chinchillas, Cameos, Shaded Silvers and Shaded Cameos, and have a similar though more recent history.

They are one of the most striking varieties with their white undercoats tipped lightly with a contrasting

Above: One of the newer breeds at shows is this pretty little British Silver Tipped Shorthair. Like all British cats they make excellent, easy-care family pets.

colour. As yet, the different colours do not have separate classes at the shows, unlike the Persian equivalents, but as these cats are sure to gain in popularity, their numbers are certain to increase. The tipping can be of any colour.

Grooming
These cats need daily combing and hand stroking like other Shorthairs. Before a show they would benefit from powdering the undercoat or from a shampoo if very dirty.

Breeding
Various breeders have reported the most unexpected crosses that have produced British Shorthair Tipped kittens, such as Siamese to Chinchilla, but the most usual is Silver Tabby Shorthair to Chinchilla and thereafter back to Chinchilla Shorthairs. With the Chocolate and Lilac Tipped the matings now would be Chocolate and Lilac Shorthairs to shorthaired Chinchillas, but they were probably developed from Kashmirs

(Longhaired Chocolate and Lilacs) to British Shorthairs.

Kittens
Because of the outcrossing to longhairs in the ancestry, the kittens have rather longer coats at birth but this disappears with the adult coat. They are charming and jolly.

SHOW SUMMARY
The undercoat should be as white as possible. The top coat should be tipped on the back, flanks, head, ears, legs and tail, with a contrasting colour to give a sparkling effect. The chin, stomach, chest and underside of the tail should be white. Tabby markings are faults. Noseleather and paw pads in keeping with the colour tipping. Eyes green in black-tipped cats; rims of eyes, nose and lips outlined in black. Eyes orange in other colours, or copper; eye rims and lips deep rose. 63 ▸

BRITISH SMOKE SHORTHAIR

These cats are the shorthaired equivalents of the Persian Smokes and have a similar breeding history. The hair for the most part is one colour, but near the roots is white or silver. Consequently, the coat appears a solid colour until the fur is parted or the cat moves.

Grooming
Daily combing and hand grooming is all that a normal shorthaired cat will require. Show cats will also need powdering to remove grease or, if they are very dirty, a shampoo a few days before a show. All powder must be brushed out.

Breeding
In order to obtain these lovely cats, it is necessary to mate Silver Tabby Shorthairs to solid coloured Shorthairs of the required colour. Thereafter Smokes are mated to Smoke and occasionally to solid Blue Shorthairs for type.

Kittens
Smoke kittens at birth look like solid coloured kittens; the lovely smoke effect is seen only as the adult coat develops.

SHOW SUMMARY
Black Smoke. Undercoat pale silvery white. The top coat heavily tipped almost to the roots with black. Long white hairs or tabby markings are faults. Noseleather black. Paw pads black or dark brown. Eyes deep yellow to copper.

Blue Smoke. Undercoat pale silvery white. Top coat heavily tipped almost to the roots with blue. No white hairs. Noseleather and paw pads blue. Eyes yellow to orange.

BRITISH TORTOISESHELL SHORTHAIR

Cats with the tortoiseshell pattern, that is, with a patched coat of black, red or cream, have been known for centuries and have appeared on the show bench ever since cats were first exhibited. In the British Shorthair, the patches show up very distinctly and are most attractive and colourful. Tortoiseshell cats are generally very sweet-natured, affectionate and gentle, with a charm all their own. They are a female-only variety, although the occasional male has occurred and one is even recorded as having sired a litter; at present, however, it is not known what factor makes 99.9 percent of tortoiseshell cats female.

Grooming
Apart from a daily combing, no special attention is necessary. Bay rum, rubbed into the coat before a show, will enhance the colours, and hand stroking will add sheen.

Breeding
Because this is a female-only variety, to produce Tortoiseshell kittens a Tortoiseshell female must be mated to a Self-coloured male of one of the required colours—black, red or cream. Even then, there is no guarantee that there will be Torties in the resultant litters. Much more research will have to be done before breeders can produce Tortoiseshell kittens unfailingly. Bicolours are not usually used as sires, as this will often give rise to Tortoiseshell-and-white (Calico) kittens as the offspring.

Kittens
Tortoiseshell kittens appear in litters with Black, Red and Cream kittens. The Tortoiseshell or Tortoiseshell-and-white kittens are always the first to be sold as they are so rare. The kittens are pretty and playful and develop early. They are usually strong, healthy and resistant to diseases and illnesses, and are not accident-prone. The markings on a kitten may not be very bright, and may be blue, pale red and dirty cream when it is very young, but when the adult coat begins to grow the blue turns to jet black, and the red and cream become clear.

SHOW SUMMARY

The coat should be evenly patched with black, red and cream, without intermingling of the colours, or any white hairs. Colour patches should be evenly distributed on the legs and face, and a facial blaze of red or cream is desirable. Noseleather and paw pads pink, black or a combination of the two. Eyes brilliant copper or orange. 105 ▶

BRITISH BLUE-CREAM SHORTHAIR

A dilute form of the Tortoiseshell, the Blue-cream is also a female-only variety. A relative newcomer to the show scene, this variety was not officially recognized in the United Kingdom until 1956, although Blue-cream kittens had appeared in litters of Blue and Cream matings and in Tortoiseshell litters (when both parents carried a gene for blue) for many years. The two palest shades of blue and cream are preferred, with no touch of red.

Below: This relaxed British Blue-Cream has a coat of mingled blue and cream hairs and orange eyes.

Grooming

Preparation for a show is relatively easy for the Blue-creams. They should be combed daily to remove dead hairs, and the coat cleaned with a little bay rum a few days before the show. Lots of hand grooming will gloss the coat.

Breeding

Blue-creams can be produced by mating a Blue with a Cream shorthair, or from Tortoiseshells. When a Blue-cream female is mated to a Cream sire, it is not possible to get Blue female kittens, but kittens of all other colours and both sexes are possible; but when mated to a Blue sire, there will be no Cream female kittens, but all other possibilities. No Blue-cream males have grown to adulthood or are known to have sired any kittens. If any appeared, it is thought that they would be sterile.

Kittens

It is not immediately apparent, when the kittens are born, which is to be a Blue-cream, and some of the best Blue-creams may look more like pale Blues at first.

SHOW SUMMARY

Coat colour should be blue and cream softly intermingled over the body, without a facial blaze. Tabby

markings and white hairs or patches are faults. Noseleather blue. Paw pads blue and/or pink. Eyes copper or orange.105 ▶

BRITISH TORTOISESHELL -AND-WHITE SHORTHAIR
(British Calico Shorthair)

Above: Black, red, cream and white make this striking Calico.

The tortoiseshell-and-white coat pattern, like the tortoiseshell, has been well known for centuries amongst alley cats, particularly in countries such as Spain, and it is always highly prized for its brilliant colouring. Again, this is a female-only variety, and the occasional male is invariably sterile. Hardy and robust, they make excellent mousers. They were formerly known as Chintz or Spanish Cats.

Grooming
A daily comb is advisable. Bay rum rubbed into the coloured patches before a show will enhance their brilliance.

Breeding
It was realized only after the Second World War that the best sires for this variety are the Bicolours, particularly those from a Tortie-and-white mother. Black-and-white or Red-and-white males are the most likely sires to produce Tortie-and-white kittens when mated with a Tortie-and-white.

Kittens
The kittens are exceptionally well balanced in temperament, happy and healthy. They develop early but the coat patches may not be very bright at first, only developing their full glory as the adult coat develops at about nine months.

SHOW SUMMARY
The coat should be boldly patched with black, cream and red with white, the patches equally balanced; white must not predominate. The tricolour patchings should cover the top of the head, ears and cheeks, back, tail and part of the flanks. Patches to be clear and well defined. A white facial blaze is desirable. Noseleather and paw-pads pink, black or a combination of the two. Eyes brilliant copper or orange 105 ▶

BRITISH BLUE TORTOISESHELL -AND-WHITE SHORTHAIR
(Dilute Calico)

There is a dilute form of the Calico or Tortoiseshell-and-white cat where blue replaces the black and cream replaces the red in the coat. Paw pads and noseleather are slate blue or pink or a combination of the two. Eyes gold.

BRITISH TABBY SHORTHAIR

The shorthaired Tabbies occur in brown, red and silver and in several coat patterns, notably the classic, mackerel and spotted. In some countries, blue and cream tabbies are also recognized.

The name 'tabby' is said to have come originally from the similarity of the cats' coat pattern to tabby or plain woven watered silk or taffeta. This type of weaving produces a striped or ridged effect on the cloth, and was known as tabbi silk in England. The word itself derives from Attabiya, a district of Baghdad where this material was made. They were also known as Cyprus Cats.

The tabby pattern is very common among domestic cats, and non-pedigree shorthaired cats are usually varieties of Brown Tabbies or 'ginger toms'. Judging from the markings of many wild felines, the original domestic tabby was probably a striped or spotted cat, and many of the cats depicted on Egyptian scrolls have spotted coats. Spotted tabbies were shown at the first cat shows, but at the beginning of this century seemed to have disappeared from the show bench, presumably because the classic tabby pattern had preference in the hearts of the breeders of the time. Fortunately, they began to make a come-back in 1965, and are now bred in the five colours, although at present only Brown, Silver and Red are recognized for competition in the United Kingdom.

It appears that the classic or blotched pattern, the most common tabby pattern in pedigree cats, is a mutation from the striped form, which first appeared in Europe among domestic and feral cats, and was already common by the middle of the seventeenth century.

Of the tabby colours, the Silver Classic Tabby is now, and seems always to have been, the most popular variety. Since the Second World War, breeding lines have been greatly improved as a result of crossing with excellent Silver Tabbies from France, and the British ones now have good type and markings.

Brown Tabbies are not common on the show bench, possibly because it is difficult to breed a cat to the required colour standard.

The fact that the name 'Red Tabby' is so often associated with the marmalade or ginger alley cat, may have contributed to the relative lack of popularity of this variety. This is a pity, as the pedigree Red Tabby in no way resembles the 'ginger tom', and is very striking with its rich red coat.

Blue and Cream Tabby Short-hairs are awaiting recognition for competition in the United Kingdom at present; Blue Tabbies are becoming popular in Europe.

Grooming
Like all shorthaired cats, Tabbies will benefit from a daily combing to remove all the dead hairs. A little bay rum, rubbed into the coat a few days before a show, imparts the rich gloss to the coat required to show the markings off at their

best. Plenty of hand stroking – with clean hands of course – will enhance the sheen and please the cat at the same time!

Breeding
Mating two Tabbies of the required colour together will give several generations of good type but then breeders sometimes mate to other self-coloured short or longhairs to improve type. Usually this will be to Blues but can also be to the solid colour in the coat pattern. Brown Tabby to a Black, Red Tabby to a Tortoiseshell, Silver Tabby to a Chinchilla, Blue Tabby to a Blue,

Below: One of the prettiest cats to be seen in this beautifully marked British Shorthair Silver Classic Tabby with immaculate coat and charming personality.

and Cream Tabby to a Cream British Shorthair or Persian (Longhair) in each case.

Kittens
Tabby kittens are born with obvious markings and usually the best marked kittens at birth become the best marked adults. However, soon after birth, the markings may fade and may then take up to six months to develop fully. Imperfectly marked kittens with white hairs or patches or incorrect coat pattern will not be suitable for showing.

SHOW SUMMARY
Classic Tabby pattern. All markings should be clearly defined from the ground colour. The characteristic head marking is a letter 'M' resembling frown marks on the forehead. Unbroken lines

run from the outer corners of the eyes towards the back of the head and there should be other pencillings on the cheeks. Lines extend back from the top of the head to the shoulder markings, which are shaped like a butterfly. Three unbroken lines run parallel to each other down the spine from the shoulder markings to the base of the tail. A large blotch on each flank is circled by one or more unbroken rings; these markings should be symmetrical on either side of the body. There should be several unbroken necklaces on the neck and upper chest, and a double row of 'buttons' running from chest to stomach. The legs should be evenly barred with narrow bracelets and the tail should be evenly ringed.

Mackerel Tabby pattern. The head is marked with the characteristic 'M', and there is an unbroken line running from the outer corner of the eyes towards the back of the head. There are other fine pencillings on the cheeks. A narrow unbroken line runs from the back of the head to the base of the tail. The rest of the body is marked with narrow unbroken lines running vertically down from the spine line. These lines should be as narrow and numerous as possible, and ideally clearly defined from the ground colour. There should be several unbroken necklaces on the neck and upper chest, and a double row of 'buttons' on the chest and stomach. The legs should be evenly barred with narrow bracelets and the tail evenly ringed.

Spotted Tabby pattern. All markings should be dense and clearly defined from the ground colour. The head should be marked with the characteristic 'M'. There is an unbroken line running from the outer corner of the eyes towards the back of the head, and there are other fine pencillings on the cheeks. Ideally, all the stripes in the tabby coat are broken up into spots, which may be round, oval or

rosette-shaped and should be as numerous and as distinct from the ground colour as possible. A dorsal stripe runs the length of the back, but it should be broken up into spots. There should be a double row of spots on the chest and stomach, and spots or broken rings on the legs and tail.

Brown Tabby. The ground colour should be a rich sable brown or coppery brown. The markings in classic, mackerel or spotted tabby patterns are dense jet black. The hind legs from paw to heel should be black. Noseleather brick red. Paw pads black. Eyes orange, hazel or deep yellow. 106 ▶

*Above: A Silver Spotted Tabby—
an outstanding looking cat with
jet black markings on pale silver.
It may be stolen for its coat.*

Red Tabby. The ground colour
should be a rich red. The markings,
lips, chin and sides of the feet dark
red. Noseleather brick red. Paw
pads deep red. Eyes deep brilliant
copper. 106 ▶

Silver Tabby. The ground colour
should be a clear silver with no
white hairs and no tinge of brown
on the nose. The chin and lips
should be silver. The markings in
classic, mackerel and spotted
patterns should be dense jet black.

Noseleather brick red or black.
Paw pads black. Eyes green or
hazel (UK); brilliant gold, orange or
hazel (US), according to different
associations. 106 ▶

Blue Tabby. The ground colour
should be pale bluish-white. The
markings in classic, mackerel and
spotted patterns should be dark
slate-blue. Noseleather rose pink.
Paw pads rose. Eyes brilliant gold.

Cream Tabby. The ground colour
should be pale cream. The
markings in classic, mackerel and
spotted patterns dark cream, but
not too hot. Noseleather and paw
pads pink. Eyes brilliant gold.

AMERICAN SHORTHAIR

Good points
- *Attractive*
- *Dignified*
- *Hardy*
- *Companionable*
- *Well balanced*
- *Good hunter*
- *Easy to groom*

Take heed
- *Likes to roam free*

This hardy cat with its tough background makes an excellent pet, not easily affected by ailments or disease. The American Shorthair is independent and likes to roam free, so may be more suited to out-of-town living than to apartment life. In the house, it will continue to 'hunt', chasing and pouncing, on whatever moves, with velvet paws.

It enjoys excursions in the open air and is typically active and curious. Being a robust natural breed, it makes a trouble-free pet with an affectionate, companionable nature. It also makes an excellent working mouser.

Grooming
The coat of the American Shorthair is very easily maintained. However, it should be combed regularly to avoid a fur ball forming in the stomach. Regular attention should also be paid to the eyes and ears to make sure they are clean and free from ear mites.

Origin and history
These cats are reputed to have come to the United States with the original settlers from Europe, who brought them on their ships, not only as companions but as working rodent officers. Every ship had its cat or cats to protect the ship's stores, and many would have left ship in the New World and been missing when it sailed again. These cats mated freely without restriction or regard for pedigree or for any colour discrimination. After years of separation from the parent European stock, they developed characteristics of their

own. Although they are still quite similar to the British Shorthair, American Shorthairs are larger, with less rounded heads and with longer noses. Years of free-ranging ancestry have also made this a hardy, fearless, intelligent breed. It was somewhat neglected as a pedigree variety until American breeders decided to breed it selectively to maintain all that is natural and lovely in their native domestic cats.

Breeding
American Shorthairs make good breeders and sensible mothers. They have endless patience.

Kittens
The kittens are confident, courageous and not prone to disease.

SHOW SUMMARY
The American Shorthair is a strong, well built cat, looking natural rather than contrived. It has the body of an athlete, built for an active outdoor life.
Coat. Thick, short, even and hard in texture. Not as plush as that of the British Shorthair and heavier and thicker in winter.
Body. Large to medium in size, lean and hard, athletic and powerful. Well developed chest and shoulders. Legs sturdy and medium in length, built for jumping and hunting. Paws full, rounded, with heavy pads. Excessive cobbiness or ranginess are faults.
Tail. Medium in length, wide at the base, tapering slightly to a blunt tip. No kinks.
Head. Large and full-cheeked.

Face bright and alert: medium long, thick, muscular neck, carrying an oval face, only slightly longer than its width. Square muzzle, firm chin. Nose medium long and uniform width. In contour a gentle curve from forehead to nose tip. Ears set wide apart, not unduly wide at the base, with slightly rounded tips.

Eyes. Large, round and wide awake. Very slightly higher on the outer edge; set wide apart.

AMERICAN SHORTHAIR COLOURS

White. Pure white. Noseleather, paw pads pink. Eyes deep blue or brilliant gold; or one deep blue and one gold in Odd-eyed Whites.

Black. Dense coal black, sound throughout coat with no rusty tinge. Noseleather black. Paw pads black or brown. Eyes brilliant gold.

Blue. One level tone of blue

Above: A Red Tabby American Shorthair. These cats prefer the outdoor life and are good hunters.

throughout, lighter shades preferred. Noseleather and paw pads blue. Eyes brilliant gold.

Red. Deep, rich clear red without shading or tabby markings. Lips and chin red. Noseleather and paw pads brick red. Eyes brilliant gold.

Cream. One level shade of buff-cream, without markings. Lighter shades preferred. Noseleather and paw pads pink. Eyes brilliant gold.

Bicolour. White with unbrindled patches of black, or blue, or red, or cream. Noseleather and paw pads in keeping with solid colour or pink. Eyes brilliant gold.

Chinchilla. Undercoat pure white. Coat on black, flanks, head and tail sufficiently tipped with black to give a characteristic sparkling silver appearance. Rims of eyes, lips and nose outlined with black. Some tipping allowed on the legs. Chin, ear tufts, stomach and chest pure white. Noseleather brick red. Paw pads black. Eyes green or blue-green.

Shaded Silver. Undercoat white with a mantle of black tipping shading down from the sides, face and tail, from dark on the ridge to white on the chin, chest, stomach and under the tail. Legs to be the same tone as the face. General effect should be much darker than the Chinchilla. Rims of eyes, lips and nose outlined with black. Noseleather brick red. Pads black. Eyes green or blue-green.107 ▶

Shell Cameo. Undercoat white. Coat on the back, flanks, head and tail to be sufficiently tipped with red to give the characteristic sparkling appearance. Face and legs may be slightly shaded with tipping. Chin, ear tufts, stomach and chest white. Rims of eyes rose. Noseleather and paw pads rose. Eyes brilliant gold.

Shaded Cameo (Red Shaded). Undercoat white with a mantle of red tipping shading down the sides, face and tail, from dark on the ridge to white on the chin, chest, stomach and under the tail. Legs to be same tone as the face. General effect to be much redder than Shell Cameo.

Black Smoke. Undercoat white, deeply tipped with black. Cat in repose appears black. Points and mask black with narrow band of white at the base of the hairs, which may be seen only when the fur is parted. Noseleather and paw pads black. Eyes brilliant gold.

Blue Smoke. Undercoat white, deeply tipped with blue. Cat in repose appears blue. Noseleather, paw pads blue. Eyes brilliant gold.

Cameo Smoke (Red Smoke). Undercoat white, deeply tipped

with red. Cat in repose appears red. Noseleather, paw pads rose. Eyes brilliant gold.

Tortoiseshell Smoke. Undercoat white, deeply tipped with black, with clearly defined patches of red and cream tipped hairs in the tortoiseshell pattern. Cat in repose appears tortoiseshell. A facial blaze of red or cream tipping is desirable. Noseleather and paw pads brick red and /or black. Eyes brilliant gold.

Tortoiseshell. Black with unbrindled patches of red and cream, clearly defined and well broken on body, legs and tail. A facial blaze of red or cream desirable. Noseleather and paw pads brick red and/or black. Eyes brilliant gold.

Calico (Tortie-and-white). White with unbrindled patches of black and red. White predominant on the underparts. Noseleather and paw pads pink. Eyes brilliant gold.

Dilute Calico. White with unbrindled patches of blue and cream. White predominant on the underparts. Noseleather and paw pads pink. Eyes brilliant gold.

Blue-cream. Blue with patches of solid cream, clearly defined and well broken on body, legs and tail. Noseleather and paw pads blue and/or pink. Eyes brilliant gold.107 ▶

Van Colours. Mostly white with colour on head, legs and tail. Noseleather and paw pads in keeping with the coloured patches or pink. Eyes should be brilliant gold colour.
Van Bicolour. Black, blue, red or cream patches on head, legs, and tail, white elsewhere.
Van Calico. Patches of black and red on head, legs and tail, white elsewhere.
Van Blue-cream. Patches of blue and cream on head, legs and tail.

Classic Tabby pattern. Markings dense and clearly defined from ground colour. Legs evenly barred. Tail evenly ringed. Several unbroken necklaces on neck and upper chest. Frown marks form letter 'M' on forehead. An unbroken line runs back from outer corner of eye. Swirls on cheeks. Vertical lines over back of head extend to shoulder markings that resemble a butterfly. Three parallel lines run down the spine from the butterfly to the tail, the three stripes well separated by the ground colour. Large solid blotch on each side should be encircled by one or more unbroken rings. Side markings symmetrical. Double row of 'buttons' on chest and stomach.

Mackerel Tabby pattern. Markings dense and clearly defined, and all narrow pencillings. Legs and tail evenly barred. Distinct necklaces on neck and upper chest. Fore-head carries characteristic 'M'. Unbroken lines run backwards from the eyes. Lines run down the head to meet the shoulders. Spine lines run together to form a narrow saddle. Narrow pencillings run around the body.

Brown Tabby. Ground colour coppery brown. Markings dense black. Lips and chin and rings

Below: The intelligent and hardy Silver Tabby American Shorthair.

around eyes paler. Backs of legs black from paw to heel. Noseleather brick red. Paw pads black or brown. Eyes brilliant gold.

Red Tabby. Ground colour red. Markings deep rich red. Lips and chin red. Noseleather and paw pads brick red. Eyes brilliant gold.

Silver Tabby. Ground colour, lips and chin pale, clear silver. Markings dense black. Noseleather brick red. Paw pads black. Eyes green or hazel. 107 ▶

Blue Tabby. Ground colour, lips and chin pale bluish-ivory. Markings very deep blue. Noseleather and paw pads rose. Eyes brilliant gold.

Cream Tabby. Ground colour, lips and chin very pale cream. Markings buff-cream, sufficiently darker than ground colour to afford a good contrast, but not dark. Nose-leather and paw pads rose. Eyes brilliant gold.

Cameo Tabby. Ground colour, lips and chin off white. Markings red. Noseleather and paw pads rose. Eyes brilliant gold.

Patched Tabby (Torbie). An established Silver, Brown or Blue classic or mackerel Tabby with patches of red and/or cream.

EXOTIC SHORTHAIR

Good points
- *Intelligent*
- *Quiet*
- *Even-tempered*
- *Playful but not destructive*
- *Sweet and loving*
- *Good with other animals and children*

Take heed
- *No known drawbacks*

If you like the docile nature of the Persian but do not have the time to groom a longhaired cat, this may be the breed for you. The Exotic Shorthair is really a hybrid breed, produced by crossing a Persian with an American Shorthair, and resulting in a 'Persian with short hair'. In looks it resembles a Persian, with its short, snub nose and wide cheeks, cobby body and short tail, yet it has a much more manageable coat. The Exotic also combines the best characteristics of both breeds, having a quiet, gentle nature and an even-tempered, sweet disposition, yet being alert, playful and responsive. It is not as destructive about the house as some of the more energetic breeds, and therefore makes an ideal pet, ever willing to please its owner.

Grooming
The Exotic Shorthair is easy to groom but the coat must be combed daily to remove dead hairs, so that too many are not swallowed and a hair ball formed in the stomach. The coat is short, but plush, so a medium-toothed comb would be best, with the occasional use of a rubber spiked brush for massage.

Origin and history
The Exotic Shorthair was deliberately developed to satisfy the desire of some breeders to have a

Persian type cat with a short coat. The results have been good. At first, Persians were mated to both American Shorthairs and Burmese, but now the cross is restricted to American Shorthairs. From 1966, these hybrids became known as Exotic Shorthairs at American shows. Earlier American Shorthairs that approximated to the Exotic in type were allowed to be re-registered as Exotics, and to keep any wins they had already gained as American Shorthairs.

Being healthy, affectionate and easy to care for, they are becoming more and more popular, and are a joy to handle in the show ring.

Breeding
To be registered as Exotic Shorthair, a cat must have one parent Persian and the other American Shorthair or both Exotic Shorthair; all colours and patterns are allowed. The queens are robust and have healthy kittens, not prone to disease or weakness.

Below: A Cream Tabby Exotic Shorthair, a Persian type cat with a more manageable coat.

Kittens
Exotic kittens are playful but not too boisterous, and they love other animals and people. They respond to gentle affectionate handling.

SHOW SUMMARY
In type the Exotic Shorthair should conform to the standard set for a Persian, but have a short, plush coat.

Coat. Medium in length, dense, soft, glossy and resilient. Not close-lying, but standing out from body.

Body. Medium to large in size, cobby and low on the legs. Deep in the chest, massive across the shoulders and rump, with a short, rounded middle. Back level. Legs short, thick and sturdy. Forelegs straight. Paws large, round and firm.

Tail. Short, thick, straight and carried low. Rounded at the tip. No kinks.

Head. Wide, round and massive, with a sweet expression. A round face on a short, thick neck. Short, broad snub nose with a nose break. Cheeks full and chin well developed. Ears small, set wide apart and low on the head, fitting into the curve of the head. The ears have rounded tips and tilt forward on the head. They are not unduly open at the base.

Eyes. Large, round, full and brilliant; set wide apart.

EXOTIC SHORTHAIR COLOURS
All colours and patterns within the American Shorthair and Persian are allowed including white, with blue, orange or odd eyes; black; blue; red; cream; chinchilla; shaded silver; chinchilla golden; shaded golden; shell cameo; shaded cameo; shell tortoiseshell; shaded tortoiseshell; black smoke; blue smoke; cameo smoke; smoke tortoiseshell; classic and mackerel tabby in silver, red, brown, blue, cream and cameo; patched tabby in brown, blue, and silver; tortoiseshell; calico; dilute calico; blue-cream; bicolour; van-bicolour; van-calico; van blue-cream and white. 108 ▶

SCOTTISH FOLD

Good points
- *Great personality*
- *Gentle and sweet*
- *Sensible*
- *Loves people*
- *Good with other animals and children*

Take heed
- *Cannot be shown in the United Kingdom*

A Scottish Fold is certainly distinctive in appearance as it wears its ears like a hat! But beauty is in the eye of the beholder and this breed has attracted criticism in some countries. The ear formation is a deformity and for this reason the Scottish Fold is not recognized for competition in the United Kingdom. However, the cat has its devotees, and is charming, sensible and good with other pets, children and strangers. It makes a good pet, does not seem to suffer any ill effects from its folded ears, and has plenty of personality.

In the United States the Scottish Fold has been bred specifically to preserve the distinctive ears, whereas in the United Kingdom the reverse is true and such features have been bred out.

Grooming
No special attention to the ears is necessary, except that they have to be kept clean. A weekly check of the teeth and a daily brush and comb will suffice to keep the coat looking neat and tidy.

Origin and history
The Scottish Fold appeared as a natural mutation from the British Shorthair in Scotland in a litter of farm cats in 1961. The first was a white cat, but the folded ear is not restricted to colour, and folds can have any coat colour or pattern. The *Universal Magazine of Knowledge and Pleasure,* published in China in 1796, refers to a cat with folded ears. They were also known in China in 1938, which shows that the gene responsible for producing folded ears has been present in the domestic cat population for at least 150 years.

Breeding
Folds mated to shorthaired domestics produce litters that contain 50

Below: A Blue-cream Scottish Fold with patched coat showing the typical head and ear set.

percent of kittens with normal (pricked) ears and 50 percent whose ears are folded downwards and forwards. Breeders recommend that Folds are mated only to normal-eared cats; Fold-to-Fold matings give rise to skeletal deformities. (cf Manx).

Kittens

The ears of Scottish Fold kittens may be only slightly folded, the definite forward folding not becoming fully apparent until they are about nine months old.

SHOW SUMMARY

The Scottish Fold is a cat of domestic shorthair type but with distinctive ears that are folded for-wards and downwards.
Coat. Thick, short, dense and soft; resilient.
Body. Medium sized, short, rounded and cobby. The same width across the shoulders and rump. Full, broad chest. Powerful and compact build. Medium length legs with neat, round paws.
Tail. Medium in length, thick at the base. Kinks, broad, thick or short tails are faults.

Above: Somewhat bizarre looking with its folded ears, the Scottish Fold is a gentle and affectionate pet. This close up shows a blue Scottish Fold.

Head. Massive and round. Well-rounded whisker pads. Short, thick neck; cheeks full, chin rounded, jaw broad. Ears wide apart and dis-tinguished by a definite fold line, the front of the ear completely covering the ear opening. Small neat ears are preferred, rounded at the tips. Nose should be short and broad, with a gentle nose break.
Eyes. Large, round, set wide apart.

SCOTTISH FOLD COLOURS

Almost all colours and coat patterns are recognized, including: solid white, black, blue, red, cream; chinchilla, shaded silver, shell cameo, shaded cameo, black smoke, blue smoke, cameo smoke; tortoiseshell, calico, dilute calico, blue-cream; bicolour; classic and mackerel tabby patterns in silver, brown, blue, cream and cameo tabby. Eye colour should be in keeping with the coat colour. 108 ▶

MANX

Good points
- *Unique appearance*
- *Intelligent and courageous*
- *Good with children and dogs*
- *Affectionate*
- *Good mouser*
- *A good office pet*

Take heed
- *Does not like to be ignored*
- *Needs daily grooming*

The Manx, or 'rumpy' as it is sometimes called, is unique in appearance. It has no tail and because the hind legs are longer than the forelegs and the back is short, it has a rabbity look and gait, and a rounded rump. The Manx is similar to the Domestic Shorthair, but has a decided hollow where the tail should be; this does not affect its balance, however, and the powerful hind legs are capable of strong, high springs. It can also run very fast. It makes a good mouser and is able to catch its own supper in the local streams (don't count on it and not feed the cat!).

The Manx makes a loyal and affectionate pet, as it is curious, intelligent and amusing, and likes to be part of the family. It may resent being left out of things or being on its own. It would make an ideal office cat because it cannot get its tail caught in doors!

Grooming
With its short, thick undercoat and soft medium length top coat, the Manx will benefit from a daily grooming session with a medium-soft brush and a medium-toothed comb to remove the dead hairs and to keep the coat shining and healthy. The ears, eyes and teeth should have regular attention too.

Origin and history
Tail-less cats have been known for centuries. Charles Darwin reported seeing them frequently in Malaysia. They also occur in Russia and China. It is possible that they were brought to the Isle of Man by ships from the Far East. However they arrived, once there they were geographically isolated, and because there were few other domestic cats on the island, the tail-lessness was perpetuated, and the gene for tail-lessness spread among the island's cats. There is a book, written 200 years ago and now in the Manx Museum at Douglas, Isle of Man, which refers to the tail-less cats of the island. They were considered lucky and appeared on jewellery, in paintings and on coins.

A state cattery on the island is now breeding Manx cats with some success, and holidaymakers can buy them to take home as souvenirs; they are also being exported. The cats were first exported from the United Kingdom to the United States in the 1930s, and they have a considerable following. It is said that King Edward VIII owned a Manx cat when he was Prince of Wales. Supreme Adult Exhibit at the British Supreme Cat Show 1979 was a magnificent Black Manx male Grand Champion.

Breeding
Manx cats are difficult to breed because like to like tail-less does not necessarily produce tail-less kittens. In fact, tailed, tail-less and stumpy-tailed kittens may result, and continuous like-to-like Manx matings result in a lethal factor coming into play, with the majority of kittens dying either before or just after birth. The tail-less gene seems to be connected with other skeletal defects, and results in other vertebrae being

fused together, giving deformed kittens with spina bifida. Frequent outcrossings to normal-tailed Shorthairs (UK) or to tailed Manx (US and UK) must be made.

Manx litters may contain the completely tail-less Manx or 'rumpy'; a 'riser', which has a very small number of vertebrae, usually immobile; a 'stubby', which has a short tail, often knobbly or kinked; and a 'longy', with a medium length tail. The show Manx must have a complete absence of tail, and, in fact, a hollow where the tail would have been. But many of the others make excellent pets and can be used for breeding with rumpies.

Kittens
Many kittens of other breeds seem to regard mother's tail as a built-in toy, but Manx kittens still seem to find plenty to play with.

SHOW SUMMARY
The principal feature of a show-standard Manx cat is the complete absence of any tail. There should be a hollow in the rump where the tail would have been. It should also have the rounded, rabbity look of a short-backed cat, with hind legs longer than forelegs and a deep flank.

Coat. Short, glossy double coat. The undercoat is thick and cottony, the top coat longer, but not too long; soft and open.

Body. A solid cat with rounded rump, strong hindquarters, deep flanks, and a short back. The hind legs are longer than the forelegs, with muscular thighs. The back arches from shoulder to rump. The feet are neat and round.

Tail. Entirely missing, with a hollow where the tail would have been. A residual tail is a fault.

Head. Large and round with prominent cheeks. Short, thick neck and a strong chin. Nose medium long, with a gentle nose dip (USA) or no nose break (UK). There are rounded whisker pads and a definite whisker break. Ears large, wide at base, tapering to slightly pointed tips (UK), rounded tips (USA). Set on top of head.

Eyes. Large, round and expressive. Set at an angle to the nose; outer corners higher than inner corners.

Colour. All colours and coat patterns, or a combination of colours and coat patterns, are permitted, except (in the United States) the chocolate, lavender and Himalayan colours and patterns or these colours with white. Colour in a Manx is a very secondary consideration after tail-lessness, shortness of back, depth of flank, and rounded rump. Eye colour should be in keeping with the coat colour. White Manx may be blue-eyed, orange-eyed, or odd-eyed (one blue, one orange). 109 ▶

Below: Despite the Manx Cat's unique appearance it makes a very intelligent, affectionate pet.

JAPANESE BOBTAIL (Mi-Ke cat)

Good points
- *Distinctive appearance*
- *Relatively non-shedding coat*
- *Intelligent*
- *Easy to groom*
- *Friendly*
- *Loyal*
- *Mixes well with other animals*

Take heed
- *No drawbacks known*

As its name suggests, the rare Japanese Bobtail is native to Japan, where it is called the Mi-Ke (mee kay) cat. Its most distinctive feature is the short bobbed tail. It is intelligent, loyal and friendly, is said to love swimming and can retrieve like a dog. It is vocal without being noisy and has a large vocabulary of chirps and meows.

Characteristically, the Bobtail will stand with one front paw uplifted in welcome, and in fact the store windows and counters in Japan often display china models of this cat with its paw lifted to welcome shoppers and passers-by. Such cats are called Maneki-neko or welcoming cats. This cat is said to mix well with other cats but to seek out members of its own breed.

Grooming
The Japanese Bobtail is very easy to maintain in perfectly groomed condition as it has a non-shedding coat and there is no thick undercoat to get tangled up. A light brushing and combing with a medium-toothed comb and pure bristle brush will suffice.

Origin and history
The Japanese Bobtail is a natural breed, native to the Far East, notably to Japan, China and Korea. Such cats have appeared in Japanese prints and paintings for centuries and even decorate a temple in Tokyo, called the Gotokuji. The cats shown are numerous and all have one paw lifted in greeting. They were first imported into the United States in 1968 but are still a rare breed.

Breeding
The Bobtail gene is recessive, and therefore a Bobtail mated to an ordinary-tailed Domestic Shorthair produces only tailed kittens. Bobtail-to-Bobtail mating, however, produces 100 per cent bobtailed kittens. No outcrossing to other breeds is necessary or permitted. Bicoloured males are the best to produce the red, black and predominantly white females.

Kittens
Japanese Bobtail kittens are lively; usually four in a litter. There is no lethal factor with Bobtails; they are usually very healthy.

SHOW SUMMARY
The Japanese Bobtail is a medium-sized cat, slender and shapely, with a distinctive bobbed tail and a decidedly Japanese set to the eyes.
Coats. Very soft and silky, single and not prone to shedding. Medium in length but shorter on the face, ears and paws. Longer and thicker on the tail than elsewhere, camouflaging the tail conformation.
Body. Medium in size, long and slender, but sturdy and well muscled. Not fragile or dainty, like some of the other Orientals, but not cobby either. Same width across the shoulders as the rump. Legs long and slender but not fragile or dainty. Hind legs longer than forelegs. Hind legs bent in stance when relaxed. One foreleg often raised. Paws oval.
Tail. The tail vertebrae are set at angles to each other and the furthest extension of the tail bone

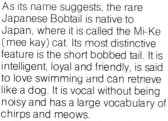

from the body should be approximately 5-7.5cm (2-3in), even though, if it could be straightened out to its full length, the tail might be 10-12.5cm (4-5in) long. The tail is normally carried upright when the cat is relaxed. The hair on the tail grows outwards in all directions producing a fluffy pom-pom effect, which camouflages the underlying bone structure.

Head. Forms an equilateral triangle, curving gently at the sides of the face. The high cheekbones give way to a distinct whisker break. The muzzle is broad and rounded, neither square nor pointed. The long nose dips gently at, or slightly below, eye level.

Eyes. Large and oval, slanted and wide apart, with an alert expression.

Colour. The preferred colour is the tricolour: black, red and white, with patches large and distinct and with white predominating. However, this is a female-only variety. Males are preferred that will give rise to this female colouring in the kittens. The only colours not allowed are the Himalayan pattern and the unpatterned agouti (Abyssinian). The more brilliant and bizarre the colours the better. White (pure glistening white), black (jet black free from rust), red (deep-rich and glowing), black-and-white, red-and-white, Mi-Ke (tricolour: black, red and white, or tortoiseshell-and-white), tortoiseshell (black, red and cream). Other Japanese Bobtail colours (known as OJBC on the show bench) include any other colour or pattern or combination thereof, with or without any other solid colour. Other solid colours include blue or cream. Patterned self colours: red, black, blue, cream, silver or brown. Other bicolours: blue-and-white and cream-and-white. Patterned bicolours: red, black, blue, cream, silver or brown combined with white. Patterned tortoiseshell. Blue-cream. Patterned blue-cream. Dilute tricolours: blue, cream and white. Patterned dilute tricolours. Patterned Mi-Ke (Tricolour). 109▶

Below: The Japanese Bobtail is a colourful, exotically different pet. Loyal and friendly, its ideal character makes it easy to mix with children and other animals.

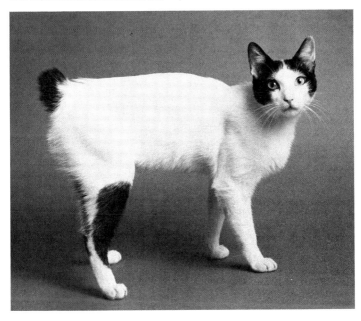

SIAMESE

Good points
- *Intelligent*
- *Smart and resourceful*
- *Companionable*
- *Takes readily to harness*

Take heed
- *Very demanding*
- *Dislikes being left alone*
- *Very vocal*
- *Needs warmth*

Judging by the number appearing at shows, the Siamese is one of the most popular breeds. It is loving and lovable, enchanting and delightful, but also exasperating, demanding and very talkative. Some Siamese seem to talk, or rather shout, all day long, and a Siamese queen when calling may be particularly trying. Prospective owners should make sure that everyone in the family is going to enjoy this boisterous temperament before deciding on the Siamese.

A Siamese will enjoy walks on harness and lead, but unlike a dog, it will rarely walk to heel! With its very extrovert personality it loves performing tricks and playing games, but dislikes being ignored and is wary and jealous of strangers and other animals.

With its terrific personality and affectionate nature, the Siamese has a tremendous following and becomes more and more popular as a pet every year.

Grooming
Easy to groom, all a Siamese needs is a twice-weekly brushing and a combing with a fine- or medium-toothed comb to remove the dead hairs. A polish with a chamois leather together with lots of hand stroking will give a shine to the coat. If greasy, give the coat a bran bath before a show

Health care
Siamese may be more prone than other cats to feline illnesses, and when ill need a great deal of attention and affection or they give up and die. To guard against illness,

they should be inoculated as early as possible, between 8 and 12 weeks of age.

Spectacle marks around the eyes or white hairs in the points are signs of ill health or distress.

Origin and history
Siamese cats are believed to have existed in Siam (Thailand) for 200 years before they finally made their way to Europe and then America in the nineteenth century. They are certainly of Eastern origin, although their exact early history has unfortunately been lost. Two of the first to come to England were thought to have been a gift to the British Consul from the King of Siam, and they were shown at the Crystal Palace, London, in 1885. The first Siamese had round faces and darker coats than those seen today, tail kinks and eye squints also being permitted at the early shows. Such 'faults' have now been bred out, and the modern Siamese does not look much like its earlier counterpart.

Breeding
Siamese are prolific breeders, having two litters a year and an average of five to six kittens in a litter, although 11 and 13 have been recorded. Siamese make good mothers as a rule though those that are highly strung are unlikely to care for their kittens when the time comes. It is therefore best not to use very nervous or bad-tempered cats for breeding.

Kittens
Siamese kittens develop early.

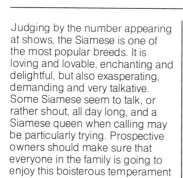

They have individual personalities very soon after birth and are precocious and self-assured. When born they are all-white, the point colour developing only gradually. In the seal and blue points, a blob of colour appears on the nose after about 10 days, but it may be three months before the chocolate and lilac points become apparent. In all colours the points are often not fully developed until a year old.

Kittens should not be taken from their mothers until they are at least 12 weeks old. They need to be with their mothers to finish their education, and if left with them for at least part of the day until this age, they always seem to be more balanced as adults.

Below: A very good Lilac-point Siamese head. Siamese in all colours are engaging pets but they do hold loud conversations!

SHOW SUMMARY

The Siamese is a medium-sized cat, long, slim, lithe and muscular, with the characteristic Himalayan coat pattern of pale body colour and darker contrasting points.

Coat. Short, fine and close-lying with a natural sheen.

Body. Medium in size, dainty, long and svelte; fine boned but strong and muscular. Not fat or flabby. Hind legs slightly longer than forelegs. Paws small, neat, oval.

Tail. Whip-like, long, thin and tapering to a point. No kinks.

Head. Long, narrow, tapering wedge with flat width between the ears. Profile straight although there may be a slight change of angle above the nose. No decided nose break. Strong chin, jaws not undershot and no whisker break. Ears very large and pointed, open at the base.

Eyes. Almond-shaped, medium in

size and slanted towards the nose. There should be the width of an eye between the eyes. No squints.

SIAMESE COLOURS

The first recorded Siamese cat was a Seal-point. The Blue-, Chocolate- and Lilac-points followed later. All appeared naturally within the breed, and are dilutions of the Seal-point, genetically. At present, these are the only colours recognized as Siamese in the United States

Coat pattern. Body should be an even pale colour, with the main contrasting colour confined to the points (mask, ears, legs and tail). The mask should cover the whole face, but not the top of the head, and be connected to the ears by tracings (except in kittens). Apparently, paler coats are easier to achieve in warmer climates, and all Siamese coats darken with age.

Seal-point. Body colour an even warm cream, slightly darker on the back, lighter on the stomach and chest. Points deep seal brown. Noseleather and paw pads seal brown. Eyes deep vivid blue. 110 ▶

Chocolate-point. Body colour ivory all over. Points warm milk-chocolate colour. Noseleather and paw pads cinnamon pink. Eyes deep vivid blue. 110 ▶

Blue-point. Body colour glacial, bluish-white, shading to a warmer white on the chest and stomach. Points slate blue. Noseleather and paws pads slate blue. Eyes deep vivid blue. 110 ▶

Lilac-point. Body colour magnolia (UK) or glacial white (USA) all over. Points frosty grey with a pinkish tone (lilac). Noseleather and paw pads lavender-pink. Eyes deep vivid blue. 110 ▶

Below: A Blue-point Siamese. All Siamese are likely to be very demanding and active. They like lots of attention and warmth.

COLOURPOINT SHORTHAIR

Basically this is a Siamese cat with point colours others than seal, chocolate, blue or lilac. Other colours have been obtained by outcrossing of Siamese to short-haired cats (British and American Shorthairs) of the required colours in order to introduce these colours into the points of the Siamese.

Although regarded as Siamese in most countries, and having the same temperament and type, because of the crossbreeding involved in their production, they are classified as Colorpoint Short-hairs in the United States. The colours recognized include red, cream and tortoiseshell points, and tabby (lynx) points in all recognized point colours.

SHOW SUMMARY
Coat pattern. Body should be an even pale colour, with the main contrasting colour confined to the points (mask, ears, legs and tail). The mask should cover the whole face, but not the top of the head, and be connected to the ears by tracings (except in kittens).

Red-point. Body clear white with any shading in the same tone as the points. Points bright apricot to deep red, deeper shades preferred, without barring. Nose-leather and paw pads flesh or coral pink. Eyes deep vivid blue.111 ▶

Cream-point. Body clear white with any shading in the same tone as the points. Points pale buff-cream to light pinkish cream without barring. Noseleather and paw pads flesh to coral. Eyes deep vivid blue.

Seal Tortie-point. Body pale fawn to cream, shading to lighter colour

Below: A Red-point Colourpoint (Siamese) Shorthair, a striking combination of clear white body, bright red points and blue eyes.

Above: A lovely Blue-cream-point Colourpoint Shorthair.

on the stomach and chest. Points seal brown, uniformly mottled with red and cream. A blaze is desirable. Noseleather seal brown or flesh pink where there is a blaze. Paw pads seal brown or flesh pink. Eyes deep vivid blue.

Chocolate Tortie-point. Body ivory. Points warm milk-chocolate uniformly mottled with red and/or cream; a blaze is desirable. Noseleather and paw pads cinnamon or flesh pink. Eyes vivid blue. 111 ▶

Blue-cream-point. Body bluish white to platinum grey, cold in tone shading to lighter colour on the stomach and chest. Points deep blue-grey uniformly mottled with cream; a blaze is desirable. Noseleather and paw pads slate or flesh pink. Eyes deep vivid blue.

Lilac-cream-point. Body glacial white. Points frosty grey with pinkish tone, uniformly mottled with pale cream; a facial blaze is desirable. Noseleather and paw pads lavender-pink or flesh pink. Eyes deep vivid blue.

Seal Tabby-point. Body cream or pale fawn, shading to lighter colour on the stomach and chest. Body shading may take the form of ghost striping. Points seal brown bars, distinct and separated by lighter background colour. Ears seal brown with paler thumbprint in the centre. Noseleather seal brown or pink edged in seal brown. Paw pads seal brown. Eyes deep vivid blue.

Chocolate Tabby-point. Body ivory, body shading may take the form of ghost striping. Points warm milk-chocolate bars, distinct and separated by lighter background colour. Ears warm milk-chocolate with paler thumbprint in centre. Noseleather cinnamon-pink or pink edged in cinnamon. Paw pads cinnamon. Eyes vivid blue. 111 ▶

Blue Tabby-point. Body bluish white to platinum grey, cold in tone, shading to lighter colour on the stomach and chest. Body shading may take the form of ghost striping. Points deep blue-grey bars, distinct and separated by lighter background colour; ears deep blue-grey with paler thumbprint in centre. Noseleather slate or pink edged in slate. Paw pads slate. Eyes deep vivid blue.

Lilac Tabby-point. Body glacial white, body shading may take the form of ghost striping. Points frosty grey with pinkish tone bars distinct and separated by lighter background colour. Ears frosty grey with pinkish tone. Paler thumbprint in centre. Noseleather lavender-pink or pink edged in lavender. Paw pads lavender-pink. Eyes deep vivid blue.

Red Tabby-point. Body white, body shading may take the form of ghost striping. Points deep red bars, distinct and separated by lighter background colour. Ears deep red, paler thumbprint in centre. Noseleather and paw pads flesh or coral. Eyes deep vivid blue.

Cream Tabby-point. Body white, shading to palest cream on the back. Points deeper buff-cream bars on white background. Ears cream with paler thumbprint in centre. Noseleather and paw pads pink. Eyes deep vivid blue.

Torbie-point. Colours and point markings as for Tabby-points, with patches of red and/or cream, irregularly distributed over the tabby pattern on the points. Red and/or cream mottling on the ears and tail permissible. Noseleather and paw pads as appropriate to the basic point colour or mottled with pink. Eyes deep vivid blue.

Below: A Chocolate Tabby-point Colourpoint Shorthair. Pretty milk chocolate on cream.

SNOWSHOE

Good points
- Striking appearance
- Good natured
- Easy to groom
- Good with children
- Alert
- Friendly

Take heed
- Vocal
- Needs human companionship

The Snowshoe is a hybrid breed produced by mating Siamese with bicolour American Shorthairs, and it therefore has the characteristics of both. It is not usually as noisy as a Siamese, but is not as quiet as most shorthaired cats. It is calm but alert and makes an ideal pet, although it should not be left alone for long periods.

Because of its origin, the Snowshoe has a modified Oriental body type, usually larger and heavier than a Siamese with less extreme features. It has a rounder head and a distinct nose break, which distinguishes it from other Siamese-derived breeds.

Grooming
Being shorthaired, the Snowshoe needs the minimum of grooming with a brush or comb to remove dead hairs. Plus hand stroking.

Origin and history
The Snowshoe is one of the newer breeds and rather like a short-haired Birman in appearance, having the Himalayan coat pattern with white feet but, unlike the Birman, it has a white muzzle, too.

There are many unregistered Snowshoes about as a result of Siamese queens mating with local bicoloured alley cats! However, the variety was considered to be so attractive that its devotees are selectively breeding these cats in the United States and a show standard is being developed.

At present only Seal-and-white and Blue-and-white are being bred, although there is no reason why the other Siamese point colours

should not be available in the Snowshoe in due course.

Breeding
Any solid colour Himalayan patterned cat without white that results from the breeding of Snowshoe with Snowshoe or Snowshoe with Siamese can be used for breeding, although it would not be eligible for competition. In this way it is hoped to build up foundation stock.

Kittens
Snowshoe kittens are lively and healthy and respond to affection. There may be three to seven in a litter. Many kittens that do not have the correct markings will be available from early matings at a reasonable price and will make excellent pets, although they cannot be shown.

SHOW SUMMARY
The Snowshoe is a modified Oriental-type shorthaired cat with white and coloured points.
Coat. Medium coarse in texture, short, glossy and close lying.
Body. Medium to large, well muscled and powerful. Long back; heavy build; males larger than females. Sleek, dainty, Oriental type is a fault. Legs long and solid with well rounded paws.
Tail. Medium in length, thick at the base, tapering slightly to the tip. Whip or very long tail is a fault.
Head. Triangular wedge of medium width and length. Obvious nose break. Round or long Siamese-like head is a fault. Neck medium in length, not thin. Ears large, alert and pointed, broad at

the base. Small or over-large ears are faults.

Eyes. Large and almond-shaped, slanted upwards from nose to ear.

SNOWSHOE COLOURS
Coat pattern. The mask, ears, legs and tail should be clearly defined from the body colour, and of the same depth of colour. The mask covers the whole face and is connected to the ears by tracings. Slightly darker shading of the body colour is allowed across the shoulders, back and top of the hips. Chest and stomach are paler. Forefeet should be white, symmetrical with the white ending in an even line around the ankle. Hind feet should be white, with symmetrical white marking extending up the leg to the heel. Muzzle should be white; the nose may be white or of the point colour. There should be no other white hairs or patches.

Seal-point. Body colour an even fawn, warm in tone, shading gradually to a lighter tone on the stomach and chest. Points, except feet and muzzle, deep seal brown. Noseleather pink if nose is white or black if nose is seal. Paw pads pink or seal or a combination of the two. Eyes deep vivid blue.

Blue-point. Body colour an even bluish white, shading gradually to a lighter colour on the chest and stomach. Points, except feet and muzzle, a deep greyish blue. Noseleather pink if nose is white, or grey if nose is blue. Paw pads pink and/or grey. Eyes vivid blue. 111 ▶

Below: A Seal-point Snowshoe, a distinctive, easy-care pet.

HAVANA BROWN

Good points
- *Attractive*
- *Agile*
- *Intelligent*
- *Active*
- *Hardy*
- *Playful*
- *Affectionate*

Take heed
- *Needs human companionship*

The American Havana Brown is a very active and highly intelligent cat. It loves people and needs human companionship and affection. It loves to play and hunt and partake in lots of other activities with the family. It is gentle by nature and makes a hardy, attractive pet.

Grooming
The medium length hair is easy to groom. A daily comb using a fine-toothed comb and a polish with a chamois leather before a show is all that is required.

Origin and history
Named Havana after its similarity in coat colour to the tobacco of a Havana cigar, the American Havana Brown has developed differently from the British (European) Havana (Self-brown Oriental Shorthair) although both had the same origins. Both were developed from a Seal-point Siamese mated to a domestic shorthair, but whereas the British Havanas were thereafter bred back to Siamese to preserve the oriental type, the American Havanas were not allowed to mate back to Siamese. This produced a less Oriental or modified Foreign type in the USA, with a shorter-wedge and medium length hair; compared with the Siamese head and very short glossy coat of the British Havana, which is in fact the same as the American Oriental Self-brown. So the American Havana has a distinctive muzzle with whisker break and nose stop and forward tilted ears comparable with no other breed. The head is

only slightly longer than wide—a true Oriental shape is a fault.

Breeding
Havana queens call loudly, clearly and frequently. They usually have four to six kittens in a litter and make good mothers. (American breeders no longer mate Havanas back to Siamese; they do not wish to perpetuate the Oriental type.)

Kittens
The kittens are very playful and agile. They are born the same colour as their parents, but their coats are a rather dull brown, and do not have the gloss of the adults. The white hairs found frequently in the kitten coat disappear when the adult coat is grown.

SHOW SUMMARY
The overall impression of the Havana Brown is of a medium-sized cat, of rich, solid colour, with firm muscle tone.
Coat. Medium in length, smooth and lustrous.
Body. Medium-sized, well muscled; medium length neck. Medium length legs; oval paws.
Tail. Medium length, tapering to a point; no kinks.
Head. Slightly longer than wide. Distinct nose break and whisker break. Chin strong. Ears large and tilted forward, with rounded tips.
Eyes. Oval; no squints.
Colour. Rich solid mahogany brown all over, solid from tip to root with no tabby markings and no white patches. Noseleather and paw pads rosy pink. Eyes pale to mid green. 112 ▶

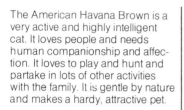

Tortoiseshell-and-white British
Shorthair 79 ▶

Tortoiseshell British
Shorthair 77 ▶

Blue-cream British
Shorthair 78 ▶

*Right: One of the newest
colours to be accepted on
the show bench is the Blue
Tortoiseshell-and-white or
Dilute Calico, where black
is replaced by blue in the
coat and red becomes cream.
These pretty kittens show the
markings to perfection. The
show standard is the same
as for the Tortoiseshell-and
-white British Shorthair.
The patches of colour
must be well defined and
equally balanced over the
top of the head, back, tail
and part of the flanks.*

Silver Spotted Tabby
British Shorthair 79 ▶

Silver Classic
Tabby British
Shorthair
kitten 79 ▶

Brown Mackerel
Tabby British
Shorthair 79 ▶

Red Classic Tabby British Shorthair 79 ▶

Left: Tabbies are one of the oldest coat patterns. Here a Brown Tabby dam with classic coat pattern is pictured with her Silver Classic Tabby kitten. The difference is in the under-coat. In the Brown Tabby it is rich sable or coppery brown; in the Silver Tabby it is clear silver. Of the three tabby colours, the Silver Classic Tabby is the most popular. Tabby patterns are common among non-pedigree cats, notably brown tabbies and marmalade cats.

Shaded Silver American Shorthair 84 ▶

Silver Classic Tabby
American Shorthair 84 ▶

Blue-cream
American Shorthair 84 ▶

Right: American Shorthairs can be any colour or coat pattern. This portrait of a Red Tabby shows the squared muzzle and firm chin which are characteristic of the breed and which, with their larger size, differentiates them from the British Shorthairs from which they originated. They are hardy and intelligent and make good pets, for although preferring the outdoor life, they are companionable and affectionate. They are also excellent mousing cats.

*Blue Classic Tabby
Scottish Fold kitten* 90 ▶

*Tortoiseshell-and-white
(Calico) Scottish Fold* 90 ▶

Shaded Cameo Exotic Shorthair 88 ▶

*Left: The slightly bizarre
looking but affectionate
Scottish Fold cat certainly
makes an excellent pet. It
has a gentle nature and is
good with other animals and
children. The one pictured
here is a Silver Tabby,
showing the typically folded
over ears. The ear formation
first appeared as a natural
mutation among British
Shorthair kittens. It is now
considered a breed in the
USA, but is not recognized
at shows in the UK because
the ears are a deformity.*

Red Tabby-and-white Manx 92 ▶

Black Manx kitten 92 ▶

Mi-Ke (Tricolour) Japanese Bobtail and kitten 94 ▶

Right: This trim little cat is a Black Manx or 'rumpy'. Its unique appearance results from the fact that it has a hollow at the back where the tail should be and its hind legs are longer than the forelegs. This gives the cat a rabbity look and gait but it does not appear to upset its balance. It can run very fast and spring high, so it makes a good mouser. Manx cats occur in all coat colours and patterns. They are loyal and like to be part of the family.

Seal-point Siamese 96 ▶

Lilac-point
Siamese
kitten 96 ▶

Blue-point
Siamese kitten 96 ▶

Chocolate-point Siamese 96 ▶

Left: The Lilac-point Siamese is a dainty looking cat with typical Siamese ways. It has frosty pink points to its Himalayan coat and the vivid blue, almond-shaped eyes characteristic of all Siamese cats.

Right: A Blue Tortie-point Siamese or Colourpoint Shorthair. This is one of the many colours recently introduced into the points of Siamese. Other new colours include Chocolate, Seal and Lilac Tortie.

Blue-point Snowshoe 102 ▶

Chocolate Tabby-
point Colourpoint
Shorthair 99 ▶

Chocolate Tortie-
point Colourpoint
Shorthair
kitten 99 ▶

Red-point Colourpoint (Siamese) Shorthair 99 ▶

Lilac Oriental
(Foreign) Shorthair 122 ▶

Havana Brown (UK)
Oriental Shorthair 122 ▶

Havana
Brown (US) 104 ▶

Left: This Oriental Brown
or Havana (UK) is a true
Oriental of Siamese shape.
On first sight it may appear
similar to the US Havana
also shown on this page and
described on page 104, both
having rich brown coats and
luminous green eyes, but the
two have quite different body
type. The US Havana is of
less extreme type as crossing with Siamese is not
now allowed. Both cats are
easy to groom. They are
both also intelligent and
need human company.

White Oriental
(Foreign) Shorthair 123 ▶

Ebony (Black) Oriental
(Foreign) Shorthair 124 ▶

Red Tipped
Oriental Shorthair 125 ▶

Right: One of the daintiest looking cats is the White Oriental Shorthair or Foreign White, a svelte and sleek cat resembling a china ornament. Unlike other white shorthair cats, the Blue-eyed White Oriental Shorthairs are not deaf. All Orientals have the same Siamese look but they come in an exceptionally wide variety of coat colours and patterns. All are a joy to own but need plenty of company, so it is a good idea to have more than one.

Egyptian
Mau Smoke 130 ▶

Silver Spotted Tabby
Oriental Shorthair 127 ▶

Chocolate (Chestnut)
Tabby Oriental
Shorthair 127 ▶

Left: A charming pair of
Oriental Chocolate Tabby
kittens, looking alert but ap-
prehensive. As with all Oriental
Shorthairs, they have pretty
ways and are easy to
groom. They are a good
choice of pet for child and
adult alike, being intelligent,
playful, active and affectionate. However, they do
demand attention and
some warmth, and since
they are more susceptible
than some breeds to illness,
kittens should be inoculated
before two months old.

Brown Burmese
(US type) 132 ▶

Red Burmese 132 ▶

Lilac Tortie
Burmese 132 ▶

Right: This Blue Burmese kitten would be very happy to be in an intelligent fun-loving household. The hallmark of all Burmese cats which make them excellent as pets is their great personality: affectionate and intelligent like the Siamese, but less vocal and destructive. They need little grooming, but plenty of hand stroking will help to keep the coat sleek and shining. All Burmese respond quickly to attention and some retrieve and even do tricks.

Natural Mink
Tonkinese 136 ▶

Bombay 138 ▶

Champagne
Mink
Tonkinese
kitten 136 ▶

Left: A Platinum Mink
Tonkinese with soft silver coat
and metallic silver points. If
you really cannot decide
between a Siamese and a
Burmese, you may consider
owning a Tonkinese since it
has some characteristics
of each of these breeds.

Right: Russian Blue kittens
are seen playing with fir
cones. They will soon grow to
become demure cats with
very gentle personalities, a
quiet voice and an unusual
preference for indoor life.

Korat 142 ▶

Russian Blue
kitten 140 ▶

Russian Blue 140 ▶

Singapura 147 ▶

Ruddy
Abyssinian kitten 144 ▶

Sorrel (Red) Abyssinian 144 ▶

Black Devon Rex
(UK eye colour) 151 ▶

Devon Si-Rex
kitten (UK) 151 ▶

Blue-cream
Cornish Rex (UK) 150 ▶

Left: This relaxed looking Ruddy or Normal Abyssinian shows quite clearly the dark ticked back and warmer orange undercoat that are characteristic of the breed. It is a lithe and muscular cat, a lover of freedom.

Right: A Tortie-and-white Cornish Rex, with evenly curled coat and whiskers. An interestingly different cat, the Rex does not seem to feel the cold despite its short coat. It is quite hardy, and a charming pet.

Black Smoke American Wirehair 152 ▶

Sphynx 154 ▶

Left: The Sphynx is the oddest looking cat and can come in all 'colours'. Unlike other cats, this usually means skin pigmentation rather than fur colour, although there is a short velvety pile on face, ears, feet and tail. Too much hair elsewhere would be considered a fault. Despite its peculiar looks it is a most affectionate, quiet, loving cat to have as a pet. It may be difficult to obtain outside Canada at present. The skin should be sponged regularly.

ORIENTAL SHORTHAIR

Good points
- *Affectionate*
- *Active and intelligent*
- *Good with children and dogs*
- *Easy to groom*

Take heed
- *Great escapologist*
- *Needs a lot of exercise*
- *Needs warmth*
- *Must be inoculated early in life*

This long-legged, sleek, svelte cat is the tomboy of the feline world. Always into everything, with its boundless energy, it will take an intelligent interest in all the family's activities and loves being taken for walks with the dogs, on or off a harness and lead. But, unlike a dog, it cannot be relied upon to obey every command or to walk to heel, particularly if something more interesting takes its attention! Because the Oriental Shorthair is energetic and has an inquisitive nature, it may be inclined to stray from home. Consequently, in towns it may be necessary to impose some restriction on its freedom for its own safety. A wired-in run, as large as you can afford, leading from a room in the house if possible, is ideal for use during the day, but it must have a range of shelves at different heights.

Since this cat may become morose if left alone for long periods, it is a good idea to have more than one, or another domestic pet for companionship. With its need for company met, the Oriental Shorthair makes the most charming and affectionate pet.

Grooming
A daily comb to remove dead hairs and a rub with a chamois leather or silk cloth is all that is required, plus plenty of hand stroking to burnish the coat. The ears and teeth should be checked regularly.

Health care
Since the Oriental Shorthair is more susceptible than some breeds to feline illnesses, it is advis-

Above: A Blue Oriental (Foreign) Shorthair, elegant and active.

able to have the kittens inoculated before they are two months old.

Origin and history
The original Oriental Shorthaired cats came from arranged matings between Siamese (for type) and other shorthaired cats (for colour). Later, Siamese were mated to longhaired Chinchillas to produce Oriental cats with tipped coats and this unusual mating combination opened up the field for all kinds of possibilities in the colour range, including new solid colours (caramel, apricot and beige), tipped tabbies, torbies (patched tabbies) and shaded, tipped and smoke tortoiseshells.

In the United Kingdom, the self or solid coloured cats are known as Foreign Shorthairs, although this name is gradually being replaced by Oriental. The tabby and other varieties are already known as Oriental Shorthairs, and in the United States, all cats of this type are known as Oriental Shorthairs. These foreign breeds had their first all foreign show in the United Kingdom in July 1979.

Breeding
Oriental queens are very prolific and can have two litters per year, often of five or six kittens each.

Kittens
The kittens are born the same colour as the adults from birth (unlike the Siamese from which they were originally derived, and whose kittens are paler at birth).

SHOW SUMMARY
Oriental Shorthairs are Siamese in type with long, svelte, lithe and muscular bodies, and long, thin tapering tails.
Coat. Short, fine, glossy and close lying.
Body. Medium-sized, long, svelte and muscular. Fine boned. Shoulders and hindquarters same width. Legs long and slim; hind legs longer than forelegs. Paws small, dainty and oval.
Tail. Long and tapering to a point, thin at the base. No kinks.
Head. Long wedge with no whisker break and no nose break. Flat skull; fine muzzle; strong chin. Neck long and slender. Ears large and pointed, wide at the base.
Eyes. Clear, almond shaped, medium in size, slanted towards the nose. No squints.

ORIENTAL SHORTHAIR COLOURS
Scientific breeding programmes have produced an exceptionally varied selection of colours and patterns within this breed.

ORIENTAL SELF BROWN
(Havana UK, Chestnut-brown Foreign)

The first all-brown shorthaired cat was exhibited in England in 1894

and called the Swiss Mountain Cat. It was believed to be a cross between a black Domestic Shorthair and a Seal-point Siamese that had resulted from an accidental mating, and the line was not perpetuated. The type, now known in the United Kingdom as Havana, was first bred in the 1950s and was the result of a planned mating between a Chocolate-point Siamese and a Domestic Shorthair of Oriental type. The name has been subject to much alteration: originally called Havana because of the likeness of the colour to Havana tobacco, the variety was actually first registered as Chestnut-brown Foreign. Exported to the United States, these cats then became Havana Browns, and in 1970 the British and European governing bodies also re-adopted the name Havana. This has caused some confusion, because the variety developed quite differently on either side of the Atlantic. In the United Kingdom and Europe the Oriental type was encouraged and the cats were outcrossed to Siamese. The American Havana Brown is a cat of less extreme type, and outcrossing to Siamese is not permitted.

SHOW SUMMARY
Coat should be a rich warm chestnut brown, the same colour from root to tip. Tabby or other markings, white hairs or patches are faults. Noseleather brown. Paw pads pinkish brown. Eyes green.

ORIENTAL LILAC
(Oriental Lavender; Foreign Lilac)

These cats were developed in the United Kingdom in the 1960s, during the Havana breeding programme. Mating two Selfbrowns (Havanas) will give rise to Lilac kittens if the parents were produced from a cross between a Russian Blue and a Seal-point Siamese. Soon, however, there will

Above: An Oriental (Foreign) Lilac head with green eyes. Orientals are easy to groom and make charming companions.

be sufficient Lilac studs for outcrosses to be unnecessary.

SHOW SUMMARY
The Oriental Lilac should have a pinkish grey coat, with a frosty grey tone: neither too blue nor too fawn. White hairs or patches, or tabby markings are faults. Noseleather, pads lavender. Eyes rich green 112 ▶

ORIENTAL CINNAMON

Originally developed from a Seal-point Siamese carrying factors for chocolate mated to a red Abyssinian. It is a lighter colour than the Havana, but similar, and is becoming popular in the United States and Europe.

SHOW SUMMARY
Coat colour should be a warm milk chocolate brown throughout, sound from root to tip. No white hairs or tabby markings. Eyes green.

ORIENTAL WHITE (Foreign White)

One of the most striking varieties, Oriental White cats look like porcelain with their smooth white coats and china blue eyes. They were developed in the 1960s and 1970s by mating white Domestic Shorthairs to Siamese. As the white coat is dominant genetically to other coat colours, it obscured the Himalayan (point restricted) coat pattern. Later, the Oriental Whites were outcrossed again to Siamese to improve the eye colour. In the early stages, green-, yellow- and odd-eyed kittens were born. Now blue is the preferred eye colour and selectively bred, Blue-eyed White Oriental Shorthairs are not deaf.

SHOW SUMMARY
Coat should be pure white throughout with no black hairs.

Noseleather pale pink. Paw pads dark pink. Eyes brilliant sapphire or china blue (UK); green or blue (USA); odd eyes not allowed on the show bench. 113 ▶

ORIENTAL EBONY (Foreign Black)

A dramatic combination of a long, svelte, jet black cat with emerald green eyes and an alert, intelligent expression.

Interest in the Black Oriental Shorthair began in the 1970s, although previously many had been bred either experimentally or accidentally, but had been sold as pets, as there was no official show standard for them.

They were originally obtained from mating Self-browns (Havanas) to Seal-point Siamese, but today as there are sufficient Oriental Black studs available, back crossing to Siamese is no longer necessary.

SHOW SUMMARY

Coat should be raven black all over from root to tip. A rusty tinge to the fur is considered a fault. Noseleather black. Paw pads black or brown. Eyes emerald green. 113 ▶

ORIENTAL BLUE (Foreign Blue)

Oriental-type blue cats have appeared from time to time in Siamese breeding programmes, but little notice was taken of them because of the other rather similar 'foreign' blue cats already established (Russian Blue and Blue Burmese). However, they appear naturally in litters of Self-browns (Havanas) and Lilacs, and they are now beginning to appear on the show bench.

SHOW SUMMARY

Coat should be a light to medium blue all over, sound from root to tip. A lighter shade of blue is preferred in the United States. White hairs or patches, especially on the chin and stomach, are faults. Noseleather and paw pads blue. Eyes green.

ORIENTAL RED
(Foreign Red)

These cats were developed from the Red-point Siamese breeding programme, at a time when Red Tabby British Shorthairs were being mated to Siamese to introduce the

red colour into the Oriental type.
They were a natural product of
these matings, but today are
obtained by mating Oriental Blacks
to Red-point Siamese. Oriental
Reds are difficult to breed without
tabby markings, so it is best to use
breeding stock without any tabby
ancestry, or markings may persist
into adulthood. It would now be
possible to use Red Burmese as
Burmese breeders have
succeeded in eradicating the
markings in the coat of the Red
Burmese. However, only British-
type Burmese should be used as
the American Burmese is rather
more cobby.

SHOW SUMMARY
Coat should be a rich, deep, clear
and brilliant red without shading or
markings. Lips and chin red. Noseleather and paw pads brick red.
Eyes copper to green; green
preferred.

ORIENTAL CREAM (Foreign Cream)

The Oriental Creams were a
by-product of the breeding
programme used to produce
Oriental Blue and Lilac Tortoise-
shells. In these programmes,
Domestic (British) Shorthaired
Tortoiseshells were mated to
Siamese and all the solid colours
appeared in the mixture. The
Cream is genetically a dilute of the
Red, and with the Oriental type,
makes a very elegant cat.

SHOW SUMMARY
Coat should be buff-cream all over
without markings, and an even
colour from root to tip. Noseleather
and paw pads pink. Eyes copper
to green; green preferred.

*Left: A sleek Oriental Ebony
(Foreign Black), one of the
newest colours on the show
bench in the UK. The first
champion appeared in 1981.
Elegant and easy to groom.*

OTHER SELF(SOLID) COLOURS

In order to produce the Shaded
Oriental Shorthairs, a Chocolate-
point Siamese male was mated to
a Chinchilla Persian female. Their
offspring were mated to Red-point
Siamese to introduce all the other
colours simultaneously. In the
process, other self-coloured cats
were produced, including Oriental
(Foreign) Caramel, a cafe au lait
colour; Oriental (Foreign) Apricot,
a Red bred from a Caramel; and
Oriental (Foreign) Beige, a Cream
bred from a Caramel. All have pale
green eyes. These are, however,
still experimental colours and
cannot be produced reliably.

ORIENTAL TIPPED

A revolution occurred with the
Orientals when the Siamese was
mated to a Chinchilla Persian in the
hope of producing Oriental-type
cats with tipped coats. The
resulting kittens were originally
mated back to Siamese for type,
but now Oriental tipped coats are
mated only to Oriental tipped in
order to preserve the coat pattern.

The tipping is similar to that of
the British Shorthair Tipped, and
such cats look very striking with
their sparkling coats. Tipping of
any colour is possible and any
colour is allowed in the United
Kingdom, including silver, cameo,
cameo tabby, blue, chestnut, lilac,
and tortoiseshell in brown, blue,
chestnut and lilac.

SHOW SUMMARY
Undercoat should be pure white.
Top coat very lightly tipped on the
back, flanks, head and tail with a
contrasting colour to give a
sparkling sheen to the coat. Chest
and underparts should be white.

Noseleather and paws pads appropriate to the tipping colour(s). Eyes according to tipping colour; green preferred.113 ▶

ORIENTAL SHADED

The Shaded Oriental Shorthairs were also developed from the Siamese × Chinchilla Persian mating. Their offspring were mated back to Siamese, Oriental Blacks or British Havanas. Thereafter, selective breeding took place to preserve the amount of tipping required. Any colour tipping is possible, and all colours are allowed in the United Kingdom, including silver, cameo, cameo tabby, blue, chestnut, lilac, and tortoiseshell in brown, blue, chestnut and lilac. Also being bred are caramel shaded silvers!

SHOW SUMMARY

Undercoat should be pure white sufficiently tipped on the back, flanks, head and tail with a contrasting colour or colours, to give the effect of a mantle overlying the white undercoat. Noseleather and paws pads according to tipping colour(s). Colour of eyes according to tipping colours but green preferred.

ORIENTAL SMOKE

Another by-product of the Siamese × Chinchilla Persian mating, the first Oriental Smoke was produced by mating a Shaded Silver to a Red-point Siamese. Today the best Oriental Smokes are mated back to Siamese, Oriental Blacks and British Havanas to preserve type. The tipping is heavy, giving the appearance of a solid coloured cat except when the fur is parted to reveal a narrow band of white hair.

Like the Tipped and Shaded Oriental Shorthairs, any colour Smoke is possible and most are now allowed for competition. These include black (ebony), blue, cameo (in red and cream), chocolate (chestnut), lilac (lavender); and tortoiseshell in brown, blue, chocolate and lilac.

SHOW SUMMARY

Undercoat should be pure white. The top coat should be very heavily tipped with a contrasting colour or colours so that the cat in repose appears of that colour(s). Noseleather, paw pads in keeping with tipping colour(s). Eyes green.

ORIENTAL PARTICOLOUR
(Oriental Torties)

The Oriental Particolours are all female-only varieties derived from the Red and Cream Oriental Shorthairs. Originally they were produced from the mating of Oriental Blacks with Red-point Siamese or Havana with Red-point Siamese, but today Oriental Torties are mated to Siamese or other solid coloured Oriental Shorthairs.

SHOW SUMMARY

Brown Tortie. Coat should be black with unbrindled patches of red and cream, clearly defined and well broken on body, head, legs and tail. A facial blaze of red or cream is desirable. Noseleather, paw pads black and/or pink. Eyes copper to green, green preferred.

Blue Tortie (Blue-cream). Coat should be blue with patches of solid cream, clearly defined and well broken on body, head, legs and tail. Noseleather and paw pads blue and/or pink. Eyes copper to green, but green preferred.

Chestnut Tortie. Coat should be chestnut brown with unbrindled patches of red and cream, clearly defined and well broken on body, head, legs and tail. A facial blaze of red or cream is desirable. Noseleather and paw pads dark and/or

Above: Many new colours are appearing amongst the Orientals, such as this Oriental Chocolate Spotted Tabby. All the elegance of an Oriental breed with a traditional coat pattern!

light pink. Eyes copper to green, but green preferred.

Lilac-cream (Lavender-cream). Coat should be lilac grey with patches of solid cream, clearly defined and well broken on body, head, legs and tail. Noseleather and paw pads pink. Eyes copper to green, but green preferred.

ORIENTAL TORBIE

Oriental Torbies (patched tabbies) appeared during the breeding programme used to obtain the Oriental Tipped, and resulted from matings between Shaded Silver Orientals and Red-point Siamese.

SHOW SUMMARY
An established brown (ebony), with patches of red, silver or chocolate (chestnut) tabby with patches of red; or a blue or lilac (lavender) tabby with patches of cream. Noseleather and paw pads patched with appropriate solid colours. Green eyes preferred.

ORIENTAL TABBY

Tabby Oriental Shorthairs were produced during the breeding programme for Tabby- (Lynx-) point Siamese, using mongrel tabbies and Siamese, and later, British Havanas mated to Tabby-point Siamese.

All colours and tabby patterns have been developed. In the United Kingdom the Spotted Tabbies were formerly called Egyptian Maus, but the name Oriental Spotted Tabby has now been adopted to save confusion with the American-bred Egyptian Mau, which is not Siamese-derived.

SHOW SUMMARY
Classic Tabby pattern. All markings dense and clearly defined. Frown lines on the forehead form the characteristic letter 'M'. Unbroken lines run from the outer corners of the eyes towards the back of the head. Other pencil-thin lines on the face form swirls on the cheeks. Lines extend from the top of the head to the shoulder markings, which are shaped in a butterfly pattern. Three unbroken lines run parallel to each other down the spine from the shoulder markings to the base of the tail. A large blotch on each flank is circled by

one or more unbroken rings; these markings should be symmetrical on either side of the body. There should be several unbroken necklaces on the neck and upper chest, and a double row of 'buttons' running from chest to stomach. Both legs and tail should be evenly ringed.

Mackerel Tabby pattern. Head is marked with the characteristic 'M'. An unbroken line runs from the outer corner of the eyes towards the back of the head. There are other fine pencil markings on the cheeks. A narrow unbroken line runs from the back of the head to the base of the tail. The rest of the body is marked with numerous narrow unbroken lines running vertically down from the spine line. There should be several unbroken necklaces on the neck and upper chest and a double row of 'buttons' on the chest and stomach. The legs should be evenly barred with narrow bracelets and the tail should be evenly ringed.

Spotted Tabby pattern (see also Egyptian Mau). Head markings as Classic Tabby. Body markings broken up into spots, which should be as numerous as possible, and may be round, oval or rosette-shaped. Dorsal stripe along the spine should be broken up into spots. There should be a double row of spots on the chest and stomach, and spots or broken rings on the legs and tail.

Ticked Tabby pattern. Body hairs to be ticked with various shades of marking colour and ground colour. Body when viewed from above to be free from noticeable spots, stripes or blotches except for darker dorsal shading. Lighter underside may show tabby markings. Face, legs and tail must show distinct tabby striping. There must be at least one distinct necklace on neck or upper chest.

Brown Tabby (Ebony Tabby). Ground colour brilliant coppery brown. Markings dense black. Eyes rimmed with black. Nose-leather black or brick red rimmed with black. Paw pads black or brown. Green eyes preferred.

Blue Tabby. Ground colour pale bluish ivory. Markings deep blue. May have warm fawn highlights over the coat. Eyes rimmed with blue. Noseleather blue or rose rimmed with blue. Paw pads rose. Green eyes preferred.

Chocolate Tabby (Chestnut Tabby). Ground colour warm fawn. Markings rich chestnut brown. Eyes rimmed with chestnut. Noseleather chestnut or pink rimmed with chestnut. Paw pads chestnut or cinnamon-pink. Green eyes. 114 ▶

Lilac Tabby (Lavender Tabby). Ground colour pale lavender

Below: An active Oriental Spotted Tabby, preparing to spring. They enjoy exercise.

(pinkish grey). Markings deep lilac-grey. Eyes rimmed with lilac. Nose-leather faded lilac or pink rimmed with lilac-grey. Paw pads lavender-pink. Green eyes preferred.

Red Tabby. Ground colour reddish apricot. Markings deep rich red. Eyes rimmed with pink or red. Noseleather brick red or pink rimmed with red. Green eyes preferred (USA); all shades from copper to green allowed (UK).

Cream Tabby. Ground colour very pale cream. Markings deep cream. Eyes rimmed with pink or cream. Noseleather pink or pink rimmed with cream. Paw pads pink. Green eyes preferred (USA); all shades from copper to green allowed in the United Kingdom breed standard.

Silver Tabby. Ground colour clear silver. Markings dense black. Eyes rimmed with black. Noseleather black or brick red rimmed with black. Pads black. Green eyes. 114 ▶

Cameo Tabby. Ground colour off white. Markings red. Noseleather and paw pads rose. Green eyes.

OCICAT

Another Siamese-derived spotted breed has been produced recently in the United States originally by crossing a Chocolate-point Siamese male with a half-Siamese, half-Abyssinian female. At present, such cats are unknown outside the United States. Except for colour, they closely resemble the Oriental Spotted Tabbies.

SHOW SUMMARY
Dark Chestnut. Ground colour pale cream. Tabby spots and markings on the chest, legs and tail dark chestnut. Eyes gold.

Light Chestnut. Ground colour pale cream. Tabby spots and markings on the chest, legs and tail milk chocolate. Eyes gold.

EGYPTIAN MAU

Good points
- *Beautiful coat*
- *Agile and playful*
- *Friendly*
- *Quiet*
- *Easy to groom*
- *Good with children*

Take heed
- *It is best to restrict freedom, as it is a prey to cat thieves*

The Egyptian Mau is the only natural breed of spotted Oriental-type cat, and since it originated in Cairo it is thought to be a descendant of the cat revered and worshipped by the Ancient Egyptians. It is shy and loving and is said to have a good memory. It is strong and muscular, can easily be trained to perform tricks, and enjoys walking on a harness and lead. This is the best way to exercise an Egyptian Mau; if allowed out too much on its own, it may be stolen for its beautiful coat.

However, being a highly active cat it should not be too confined. The best solution if you cannot take the cat for walks yourself is to construct a wired-in pen in the garden, complete with roof and some means of access to the owner's house or a shelter to retreat from rain or too much sun. It adores people and should not be shut up on its own for long spells.

Grooming
As with all shorthaired cats, little grooming is required, although the Mau will benefit from and enjoy a daily brushing and combing to remove dead hairs, which it might otherwise swallow. Before a show, a little bay rum should be used. Do not use powder as this would mar the spots on the coat.

Origin and history
Thought to be the original domestic cats of Ancient Egypt, spotted cats or their descendants are depicted in early Egyptian art and symbolized in the gods Ra and Bast, both of whom were personi-

Above: A lovely, almond-eyed Silver Egyptian Mau from America.

fied as cats. The name 'Mau' is simply the Egyptian word for cat.

The Egyptian Mau has been developed principally in the United States, and the similar spotted cats formerly called Egyptian Maus in the United Kingdom are now known as Oriental Spotted Shorthairs, as they are a Siamese-derived breed.

The first Egyptian Maus to be seen in Europe appeared at a cat show in Rome in the mid 1950s, and from there were taken to the United States in 1956. They were shown at the Empire Cat Show in 1957, attracting great interest.

Breeding
Since the Mau is a natural breed, outcrossing to other breeds is not permitted. With the original stock four colours have now been developed. The queens make excellent mothers; they are good tempered, quiet and devoted. The gestation period for Egyptian Maus is reputed to be 63-73 days!

Kittens

Egyptian Mau kittens are born with obvious spots, and are active and playful from the start. There are usually four to a litter.

SHOW SUMMARY

The Egyptian Mau is halfway in appearance between the svelte Oriental type and the cobby Domestic Shorthair. Egyptian Maus are alert, well balanced, muscular and colourful.

Coat. The fur is dense, resilient and lustrous, medium long, silky, fine.

Body. A modified Oriental type; medium in length, graceful and muscular, especially the males. Hind legs are longer than forelegs, and give the appearance that the cat is standing on tip-toe. The paws are small and dainty, round to oval.

Tail. Medium long, wide at the base, tapering slightly. A whip tail is considered a fault.

Head. A rounded wedge without flat planes. There is a slight rise from the bridge of the nose to the forehead, but no nose break. Ears large and wide apart, broad at the base, moderately pointed, with or without ear tufts. Small ears are considered a fault.

Eyes. Large, almond shaped. Small, round or Oriental eyes are considered a fault.

EGYPTIAN MAU COLOURS

Coat pattern. There should be a good contrast between the pale ground colour and the spots. Each hair carries two bands of colour and the pigmentation of spots and stripes can be seen both in the fur and in the skin.

The forehead is marked with the characteristic 'M', and other marks form lines between the ears that continue down the back of the neck, ideally breaking into elongated spots along the spine. As the spinal lines reach the hindquarters, the spots merge to form a dorsal stripe which continues along to the tail tip. Two darker lines across the cheeks, almost meeting. The chest has one or more necklaces, preferably broken in the centre. The shoulder markings may be stripes or spots. The front legs are heavily barred. Markings on the body should be spotted, the spots varying in size and shape; round, even spots are preferred. Spots should not run together in a broken, mackerel pattern. The hindquarters and upper hind legs should carry spots and stripes; bars on the thighs and back, spots on the lower leg. There should be 'vest button' spots

Silver. Ground colour light silver, lighter on the undersides. Markings charcoal grey. Backs of ears greyish pink, tipped in black. Toes black, colour extending up the backs of the hind legs. Nose, lips and eyes rimmed in black. Noseleather brick red. Paw pads black. Eyes gooseberry green.

Bronze. Ground colour honey bronze, shading to pale creamy ivory on undersides. Markings dark brown. Backs of ears tawny pink edged with dark brown. Paws dark brown with dark colour extending up the backs of the hind legs. Nose, lips and eyes rimmed with black or dark brown. Bridge of the nose ochre coloured. Noseleather brick red. Paw pads black or dark brown. Eyes gooseberry green.

Smoke. Ground colour charcoal grey with silvery white undercoat. Markings jet black. Paws black, with black extending between the toes and up the backs of the hind legs. Nose, lips and eyes rimmed with black. Noseleather and paw pads black. Eyes gooseberry green. 114 ▶

Pewter. Ground colour pale fawn. Each hair on the back and flanks ticked (banded) with silver and beige, tipped with black, shading to pale cream on the undersides. Markings charcoal grey to dark brown. Nose, lips and eyes rimmed with charcoal to dark brown. Noseleather brick red. Paw pads charcoal to dark brown. Eyes gooseberry green.

BURMESE

Good points
- *Great personality*
- *Good with children*
- *Highly intelligent*
- *Playful*
- *Elegant*

Take heed
- *Very adventurous, may wander*
- *Needs some warmth*
- *Needs company*

The Burmese makes an excellent pet. It has a sleek, shorthaired coat that is very easy to groom, is more intelligent and more affectionate than many cats, but above all has a fantastic personality. It just loves people and is very good with children, but it does not like to be left alone. If you are out all day, then it is better to have two, so that they are company for each other. One cat is fun, but two cats are fun squared, especially Burmese!

The Burmese is tomboyish by nature, although many people consider the smooth shining coat and yellow eyes to be the height of elegance. This cat will always give a grand, bouncy welcome to the stranger, and time and affection devoted to this breed more than repays the owner in loyalty and affection. Beautifully behaved with the children, a Burmese loves to sleep in human beds if it gets the chance. There is usually little harm in this practice and both child and cat seem to appreciate the added warmth and friendship.

Grooming
The Burmese is one of the easiest cats to groom. A very fine-toothed comb used once or twice a week will remove dead hairs and be appreciated by the cat, as will plenty of hand stroking. For show cats, a bran bath a few days before the show will absorb any excess grease in the coat. However, the glossy Burmese coat is obtained only by keeping the cat in perfect condition; a healthy Brown Burmese should look like polished mahogany.

Origin and history
Although cats resembling the Burmese have been recorded in books from Thailand dating back to the 15th century, the breed as we know it today was developed in the United States in 1930, when a brown female cat of Oriental type, named Wong Mau, was imported

Below: A sleek-coated Blue Burmese. Any coloured Burmese cat is a joy to own.

Above: The original coloured Burmese—an elegant mahogany.

to the West Coast from Burma. As there were no similar cats for her to mate with, she was mated to a Siamese. All the kittens born were therefore hybrids, but when they were mated back to their mother, brown kittens resembling the mother were produced. The personalities of these cats were so much admired, being as affectionate and as intelligent as the Siamese but less vocal and less destructive, that the breed soon became very popular.

The first Brown Burmese were imported into the United Kingdom in 1948, and this breed is now one of the most numerous on the show bench; indeed they now have their own all-Burmese shows. Of the other colours, the Blue was the first to appear in the United Kingdom (1955) and was such an unexpected event that the first kitten was registered as 'Sealcoat Blue Surprise'. Since then, with intensive breeding programmes, Lilac, Cream, Red, Chocolate and Tortie Burmese have been produced, all having the same lovable temperament.

In some American Associations the Blue, Chocolate (Champagne) and Lilac (Platinum) Burmese colours are considered a separate breed known as the **Malayan,** as they were derived from other coloured shorthairs.

Breeding
The Burmese is more prolific than most cats. A queen usually has large litters— sometimes of up to 10 kittens, although four or five is the average number. Burmese make excellent mothers, bringing their kittens up very strictly with definite ideas on good manners.

Kittens
The kittens are exceptionally active and playful. They are born with much paler coats than the adults, and in the case of the Brown Burmese, mother and kittens look

like plain and milk chocolate together. It is often difficult to assess the exact shade of the paler coated Burmese at birth, because the final coat colour takes some weeks to develop, as does the eye colour. Due to increasing demand, you may have to wait for one.

SHOW SUMMARY

The Burmese is a medium-sized cat of modified Oriental type with a muscular frame and heavier build than its looks would suggest. The British Burmese is slightly less rounded and cobby than the American Burmese, with longer and more slender legs.

Coat. Fine, sleek and glossy, short and close-lying.

Body. A medium-sized cat, hard and muscular; chest rounded and back straight; legs long and slender, hind legs slightly longer than forelegs; paws neat and oval (UK), round (USA).

Tail. Medium in length and tapering slightly to a rounded tip. Not whip-like or kinked.

Head. Slightly rounded on top between the ears, which are wide apart. The high, wide cheekbones taper to a medium-blunt wedge (UK); slight taper to a short, well developed muzzle (US). Chin firm; a jaw pinch is a fault. Ears rounded at the tips and open at the base, with a slight forward tilt in profile.

Below: A Blue Tortie Burmese, its coat patched with blue and cream.

The nose is medium in length with a distinct break in profile. Face should have a sweet expression.
Eyes. Oriental in shape along the top line and rounded underneath (UK); rounded (USA). Large and lustrous, set well apart.

BURMESE COLOURS

Brown was the first colour to be bred and recognized and is often considered the most attractive. Brown Burmese have been exported to many countries, from both the United Kingdom and the United States, and have immediately become popular everywhere. Although selective breeding in the United Kingdom has produced several colour varieties, in the United States only Sable (Brown), Blue, Champagne (Chocolate) and Platinum (Lilac) are recognized for competition.

Brown (Sable). Adult colour should be an even dark chocolate or sable brown, shading very slightly to a lighter tone on the underparts. Noseleather and paw pads brown. Eyes deep yellow to gold, with no tinge of green. 115 ▶

Blue. Adult colour should be soft silver-grey, shading to a paler tone on the underparts. Ears, face and feet have a silver sheen. Noseleather dark grey. Paw pads grey. Eyes deep to golden yellow preferred, although a greenish tinge is acceptable.

Above: A Chocolate Tortie Burmese may display two shades of red and chocolate, mingled or blotched, and a facial blaze.

Chocolate (Champagne). Adult colour should be a warm milk chocolate all over, with slightly darker shading on the points permitted. Noseleather warm chocolate brown. Paw pads brick red to chocolate brown. Eyes deep to golden yellow.

Lilac (Platinum). Adults should be a delicate dove grey with a pinkish tinge. Ears and mask are slightly darker. Noseleather and paw pads lavender-pink. Eyes deep or golden yellow.

Red. Adults should be light tangerine in colour. Ears are slightly darker. Noseleather and paw pads pink. Eyes deep or golden yellow. 115 ▶

Cream. Adults should be a rich cream. Ears only slightly darker.

Noseleather and paw pads pink. Eyes deep or golden yellow.

Brown Tortie. Adults should have brown and red patches without any barring. Noseleather and paw pads plain or blotched brown and pink. Eyes deep or golden yellow.

Blue Tortie. The adult coat should have patches of blue and cream without any barring. Noseleather and paw pads plain or blotched blue and pink. Eyes deep or golden yellow.

Chocolate Tortie. Adult coat should have chocolate and red blotches without barring. Noseleather and paw pads plain or blotched chocolate and pink. Eyes deep or golden yellow.

Lilac Tortie. Adult coat should have lilac and cream blotches without barring. Noseleather and paw pads plain or blotched lilac and pink. Eyes should be deep or golden yellow. 115 ▶

TONKINESE (Tonkanese)

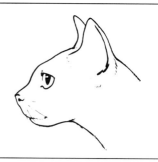

Good points
- *Friendly and affectionate*
- *Easy to groom*
- *Good with children*
- *Active and full of fun*
- *Loves people*
- *Takes happily to harness*

Take heed
- *Curious, so may get lost*
- *Not afraid of traffic*

The Tonkinese is a hybrid breed, a cross between the Siamese and the Burmese, and — as would be expected — it has some characteristics of each of these breeds. Because it loves people, it is apt to associate cars with people and lie down in front of them! Because of its curious nature, it goes for long walks and sometimes gets lost or risks meeting with a traffic accident. It should, therefore, have some restrictions to its freedom, although it would be cruel to confine it to a small and uninteresting room or cage. An ideal place for a Tonkinese to exercise during the day or during the owner's absence is a large, wired-in run with a roof, about 2m (6ft) high, and with lots of shelves at different heights. The cat will amuse itself for hours, running up and down and jumping from one shelf to the next, or just sit dozing in the sun at high level, keeping an eye on intruders into its garden. Some shelter should also be provided against the rain or too much sun.

Grooming
The Tonkinese is an easy cat to groom. All it needs is a fine-toothed comb, and perhaps a rubber spiked brush for massage. A bran bath just before a show will remove any excess grease from the coat, and a silk cloth or chamois leather will give it a polish. The ears should be inspected regularly for mites, and the outer ear only can be wiped out with a cotton wool bud when necessary. Avoid probing too deeply when cleaning the ears.

Origin and history
This breed was developed in the 1960s and 1970s, mainly in the United States and Canada, although all over the world, no doubt, breeders with both Siamese and Burmese have experienced attractive cross-bred kittens and considered perpetuating them. The Tonkinese was finally accepted as a breed in the USA in 1975, although from the European view it is not strictly a breed at all.

Breeding
Tonkinese, or Tonks as they are affectionately known, are bred now only to Tonks in the USA, giving 50% Tonks, 25% Siamese and 25% Burmese. The non-Tonk kittens from these matings cannot be shown because their pedigrees are not pure, but they make excellent pets. The first cross of Siamese to Burmese gives 100% Tonkinese.

Kittens
Tonkinese kittens are born paler in colour than their parents, the adult colour gradually developing.

SHOW SUMMARY
The Tonkinese is an Oriental-type cat, medium in size, lithe and well-muscled.
Coat. Soft and close-lying with a natural sheen.
Body. Medium-sized, well muscled, with long legs, the hind legs slightly longer than the forelegs. The slim legs terminate in small, dainty, oval paws.
Tail. Long and tapering from a thick base to a thin tip. No kinks.

Above: One of the early British Tonkinese, although it is not accepted as a breed in the UK because it does not 'breed true'.

Head. A modified wedge with a square muzzle. In profile there is a slight nose break. A medium long neck, but not as long as that of a Siamese. Ears medium in size, pricked forward and rounded.
Eyes. Almond-shaped, set wide apart.

TONKINESE COLOURS
Four colours are accepted. The adult coat should be a solid colour, shading to a slightly lighter tone on the underparts, and with clearly defined points.116 ▶

Natural Mink. A warm brown with dark chocolate points. Noseleather, paw pads brown. Eyes blue-green.

Honey Mink. A warm, ruddy brown, with chocolate points. Noseleather and paw pads mid-brown. Eyes blue-green.

Champagne Mink. A soft, warm beige, with light brown points. Noseleather and paw pads cinnamon-pink. Eyes blue-green.

Blue Mink. A soft blue to blue-grey, with light blue to slate blue points. Noseleather and paw pads blue-grey. Eyes blue-green.

Platinum Mink. A soft silver body with metallic silver points. Nose-leather lilac and paw pads pink. Eyes blue-green. 116 ▶

BOMBAY

Good points
- *Striking appearance*
- *Delightful personality*
- *Even-tempered*
- *Reasonably quiet*
- *Mixes well with other cats, children and dogs*
- *Easy to groom*

Take heed
- *Does not like to be ignored*

The Bombay has been described as a 'mini black panther' with a coat of patent leather and copper penny eyes. It has an ideal temperament and personality. It is hardy, affectionate and contented, and seems always to be purring.

The Bombay is very easy to groom because of its sleek coat, and so makes an ideal pet in many ways. However, it does not like to be ignored, and therefore should not be left alone for hours at a time, deprived of human companionship. It is good with children and mixes well with other animals. It loves people and much activity, and it would be cruel to own only one if you have to be out all day.

Grooming
The close-lying coat needs

combing daily with a very fine-toothed or flea comb to remove dead hairs; the show animal can be polished with a silk cloth or chamois leather. The cat might also enjoy a bran bath occasionally. Much hand stroking is appreciated, but please no hand-cream, which can spoil the whole effect! Ears and eyes should be examined regularly.

Origin and history
The Bombay is a man-made breed, produced by crossing Brown (Sable) Burmese with Black American Shorthairs, and the resultant cat has the black colour and hardiness of the American Shorthair and the sleek glossy coat, intelligence and affection of the Burmese.

Breeding
The Bombay, although developed

as a hybrid, is found to breed true, and Bombay × Bombay produces 100 percent Bombay kittens. In the original crosses black was the dominant colour, and so even with the first cross, all the kittens could be registered as Bombay. Since then type, colour and eye colour have been maintained by careful, controlled breeding programmes. The queens make good sensible mothers, and they mature early from kittenhood.

Kittens
The kittens are lively, full of energy and very affectionate and trusting. They need companionship and should not be neglected. Kitten coats may be rusty coloured at first, maturing to pure black.

SHOW SUMMARY
More show points are given to the coat condition and colour in this breed than in any other, as the coat is considered to be more important even than the type.

Coat. Very short and close-lying with a patent leather sheen or satin finish. It most resembles the Burmese coat.

Body. Medium in size, and muscular, neither cobby nor rangy. Males larger than females. Females more dainty. Legs medium long.

Tail. Medium long, straight, no kinks.

Head. Rounded, without any flat planes. Face wide, with a good width between the eyes. Short, well-developed muzzle. Nose broad with a distinct nose break. Ears rounded, medium in size and alert. Broad at base, set wide apart on curve of head, tilted forward.

Eyes. Round, and set wide apart.

Colour. Black to the roots without white hairs or patches. Nose-leather and paw pads black. Eyes new penny copper, deep and brilliant. Gold eyes sometimes accepted, but not green. 116 ▶

Left: A Bombay has a distinctive head with very large eyes. It is delightfully even-tempered and loving as it is derived from both American Shorthair and Burmese.

RUSSIAN BLUE (Maltese)

Good points
- *Sweet and quiet*
- *Gentle and shy*
- *Companionable*
- *Easy to groom*
- *Takes well to apartments*
- *May accept a harness and lead*

Take heed
- *Because of the small voice the queen may call without notice*

Whatever else is red in Russia, Russian cats are blue! The outstanding feature of the Russian Blue is its quiet sweetness. It is shy and gentle, and makes a loving, agreeable companion. It will become very attached to its owner, is willing to please, and seems to take easily to living in an apartment, in fact preferring an indoor life. Its blue plush coat is different from that of any other breed and somewhat seal-like in texture. The guard hairs are tipped with silver, which gives a silver sheen to the coat, enhancing the look of this lovely, docile cat.

The only disadvantage of this breed is that its voice is often so quiet that breeders may find it difficult to tell when a queen is calling; but because this cat is not prone to roam away from home, it is less likely to mismate with the local tom cats than many other breeds. If it is shut in somewhere this quietness may prevent the cat from being rescued.

Grooming
The Russian Blue is easy to groom, as the fur is very short and plush. It needs only an occasional brushing and a combing with a fine-toothed comb, and a polish with a chamois leather or an ungreasy hand. A show cat may be given a bran bath before the show to absorb any excess grease from the coat.

Origin and history
It is rumoured that the original cats came from Archangel in the USSR, brought to England by British sailors visiting the port. Before 1900, they were known as Archangel Blues, but also as Maltese and Spanish cats, and there seems to have been some confusion as to what was or was not a Russian Blue, although the fact that there are many of these cats in Scandinavia is supportive evidence of a Russian origin.

They were shown in the United Kingdom at the end of the nineteenth century, but as there were so few cats to mate them with, they were outcrossed to British Blues and Blue-point Siamese. This was nearly the death of the breed and had very undesirable results, particularly in the loss of the distinctive coat. After the Second World War every effort was made in the United Kingdom to reinstate this breed and now much better specimens are appearing.

Breeding
Russian Blues usually have one or two litters a year, with an average of four or five kittens to each. Finding appropriate breeding stock is still a problem, especially in the United States, where there are very few. Unfortunately it seems to be very difficult to breed a cat with both good type and a good coat.

Kittens
Russian Blue kittens are born with fluffy coats and may have faint tabby markings until the adult coat develops.

Right: A charming portrait of a Russian Blue mother and four kittens. Shy and gentle, they make excellent pets for the elderly.

SHOW SUMMARY

The Russian Blue is a medium-to-large cat of Oriental type, lithe and graceful with a short, dense, plush coat.

Coat. Very short and dense. Very plushy, silky and soft, resembling sealskin.

Body. Long, lithe and graceful. Medium-strong bones. Long legs with small oval paws (UK); rounded (USA). Hind legs longer than forelegs.

Tail. Long and tapering, thicker at the base.

Head. Wedge-shaped, shorter than that of a Siamese, with a receding forehead. Straight nose and forehead with a change of angle above the nose. Flat, narrow skull. Prominent whisker pads.

Strong chin. Neck long and slender but appearing shorter because covered with thick, short plush fur. Ears pointed, large and wide at the base, set vertical on the head. Almost transparent, and without ear tufts.

Eyes. Almond in shape and set wide apart, slanting to the nose.

Colour. A clear all-over blue, without shading or white hairs but with silver tipped guard hairs giving the whole coat a silvery sheen. A medium blue colour is preferred in the UK and a paler blue in the USA. Black Russians and White Russians are now being bred, particularly in New Zealand. Noseleather and paw pads slate blue. (Paw pads lavender-pink in USA.) Eyes bright, vivid green. 117 ▶

KORAT

Good points
- *Pretty*
- *Quiet*
- *Sweet and gentle*
- *Intelligent*
- *Not destructive*
- *Good with other animals*

Take heed
- *Does not like loud or sudden noises*

The Korat has been described as having 'busy charm'. It loves to be petted, is smart, and likes energetic games. It dislikes sudden noises, however, and so would be best suited to a quiet, well-ordered household, rather than a mad house of boisterous children.

The Korat likes quiet, gentle people and gets very attached to its owner. It will get on well with other cats of different breeds, but prefers its own breed. It will also settle happily with a docile dog, provided it is introduced gently. The Korat is not too talkative, except when 'calling', and would make an ideal pet for someone wanting a sweet, loving, quiet companion.

However, it is still a rare breed, and you may have to wait for a kitten. At present there are more in the United States than elsewhere,

Below: A Korat in playful mood. These pretty blue cats with green eyes are gentle, quiet, sweet and companionable. A joy to own.

but they are now being bred in the United Kingdom, Canada, South Africa, Australia and New Zealand, and are becoming popular.

Grooming
The Korat's single coat is very easy to keep in perfect condition. All it needs is a daily combing to remove dead hairs, so that the cat does not swallow them, and a polish with a chamois leather or silk cloth. It will enjoy lots of hand stroking, which will be good for the coat and make it shine.

Origin and history
The Korat is a natural breed, native to the Korat plateau in Thailand. Since 1959, several have been imported into the United States, and some began to arrive in the United Kingdom from America in 1972, although one specimen was apparently shown in England as early as 1896 at the National Cat Show; it was then thought to be a Blue Siamese but later was realized to be a Korat.

In the town of Korat these cats are known as Si-Sawat, which means 'good fortune'. In Thailand it is often called 'the cloud-coloured cat with eyes the colour of young rice'. One Thailand travel poster shows a girl in native Thai costume holding a Blue Korat cat. They are prized in their homeland, and a pair given to a bride means a fortunate, prosperous and happy marriage. The males are fearless fighters.

Korats have been known for hundreds of years in Thailand as is proved by a book of cat poems from the Ayudhya period (AD1350-1767), in which three cats are referred to: the Seal-point Siamese, a copper-coloured cat (probably Burmese) and the Korat. They have now spread to all parts of the world where pedigree cats are bred and shown.

Breeding
When a kitten is sold, the new owner has to promise to neuter (alter) a kitten at the age of six months, or to mate it only to another Korat. This is to keep the breed as pure as it is, without contamination from other breeds. Korat queens make good mothers, very meticulous and clean, and the average Korat litter usually contains three or four kittens.

Kittens
The kittens are born the same colour as the adults, the beautiful silver grey coat present from the start. Kittens often have amber eyes, and the adult eye colour may take from two to four years to develop fully.

SHOW SUMMARY
The Korat is a medium-sized, strong and muscular cat. The males are more powerful than the females.

Coat. Single, short, glossy, fine and close lying. Extra short and fine on the back of the ears, nose and paws.

Body. Medium-sized, strong and muscular, semicobby with a rounded back and lying low on the legs. The forelegs are slightly shorter than the hind legs. Paws oval.

Tail. Medium long, tapering to a rounded tip.

Head. Heart-shaped head and face with a semipointed muzzle, a strong chin and jaw, and a large flat forehead. The nose is short with a downward curve above the tip of the nose. Gentle nose break. Ears alert with rounded tips, medium large, set high on head; open at the base; only slight interior furnishing.

Eyes. Prominent, over-large, luminous and set wide apart. Round when open, with slight slant when closed.

Colour. Silver-blue all over, tipped with silver to give a sheen, especially intense on backs of the ears, nose and paws. There should be no white hairs, spots or tabby markings. Noseleather dark blue or lavender. Paw pads dark blue or lavender with a pinkish tinge. Eyes brilliant green; amber tinge permitted in kittens. 117 ▶

ABYSSINIAN

- Affectionate
- Playful
- Quiet
- Loving
- Good with children
- Easy to groom

Take heed
- Very active
- Dislikes confinement
- Unsuitable for an apartment

The Abyssinian is a highly intelligent cat, capable of showing a degree of obedience that is rare in cats. It is responsive to affection and likes to be part of the family. It can be easily trained to do tricks with its paws and to retrieve.

An Abyssinian looks like a little wild cat, and this appearance, coupled with its responsive personality, makes the cat particularly appealing to men. Men who think they do not like cats often succumb to the charm of an Abyssinian.

Because of its active nature, the Abyssinian prefers an outdoor life and dislikes being confined to a small area or caged in a cattery. It is best not to have an Abyssinian unless you live in the country or have a large garden.

Generally strong and healthy, feline leukaemia has taken its toll of the breed in the past, and it is best to obtain a leukaemia-free kitten. There is currently no cure for this virus disease.

Grooming

An Abyssinian is very easy to groom. It is advisable to brush daily to remove any dead hairs. A shorthaired soft bristle brush or rubber brush is ideal and a very fine-toothed comb with a handle will remove loose hairs and double as a flea comb if necessary. For show cats, a little bay rum and a rub with a chamois leather will show off the coat to advantage. Daily hand stroking will gloss the coat, and be loved by the cat. The teeth and ears should also be checked regularly.

Origin and history

The early Abyssinian-like cats were known as hare or rabbit cats because of the similarity of their ticked coats, and they were also shown as Russian and Spanish cats at the early shows in the United Kingdom. Rabbit fur, however, has only a single band of colour (ticking) on each hair, whereas a good Abyssinian will have two or three bands of darker colour on each hair (double or treble ticking), with the pale colour next to the skin.

Because of its likeness to pictures of Ancient Egyptian cats, it has been claimed that the Abyssinian originates from the sacred cats of Egypt, but it is much more likely that breeders, impressed by this likeness, decided to perpetuate these features by judicious breeding. The Romans are known to have taken cats from Egypt and to have brought them to England, so the genes necessary to produce the 'Egyptian look' could have been introduced into Britain in this fashion. They would then be preserved within the British domestic cat population until someone wished to isolate them again by careful and selective breeding. All British Abyssinians are descended from other British cats, and all American Abyssinians can trace their origins to British imports after 1907.

Abyssinians were first recorded in Britain in 1882, and by 1970 all countries in the world had recognized the Abyssinian as a true breed. In 1979, which was the Golden Jubilee year of the UK

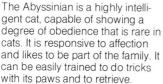

Abyssinian Cat Club, the first all-Abyssinian cat show was held in Gloucester, England. Abyssinians are one of the most popular short-haired breeds in the United States, also. They are well represented in excellent competitive classes at the shows, and take many high honours, in both shorthair and all-breed championships.

Breeding
Abyssinians have never been numerous and usually have only three or four kittens to a litter, mostly males. Selective breeding and outcrossing to other breeds to obtain new colours will undoubtedly bring stamina to the breed. The queens are usually attentive mothers, interested in their offspring.

Kittens
Abyssinian kittens usually mature early and are fearless and playful. They arch their backs and purr loudly, demanding attention. It may take 18 months before the coats develop their full adult beauty.

SHOW SUMMARY
The Abyssinian is medium-sized, of modified Oriental type, firm, lithe and muscular with a distinctive ticked coat.

Coat. Short, fine and close-lying, lustrous and resilient.

Body. Medium-sized, slender and lithe, solid and muscular. Oriental in type, though not as extreme as a Siamese. Medium length, slim, fine-boned legs with small oval paws; characteristic stance as if on tip-toe.

Tail. Medium long, broad at the base and tapering. Not whip-like and no kinks.

Head. Medium broad, slightly rounded wedge on an elegant arched neck. Muzzle not sharply pointed. Ears wide apart, broad at the base, well cupped and tufted. Chin firm; slight nose break in profile.

Eyes. Set wide apart and expressive. Slightly slanted in setting, almond in shape.

Below: An active Ruddy (or Normal) Abyssinian. A lovely, quiet breed.

ABYSSINIAN COLOURS

Originally only two colour varieties were recognized within this breed, the Ruddy and the Red (now Sorrel), and these are the only two colours accepted for competition in the United States at present.

A Blue Abyssinian also occurs naturally within the breed and was recognized in the United Kingdom in 1975. Now several other colours are appearing in the Assessment classes, including Lilac, Chocolate, Silver, Tortie, Red and Cream, although all these are the results of outcrossing to other shorthaired cats for colours.

Ruddy (Normal). Coat rich, rufous red, ticked with two or three bands of black or dark brown, with a paler orange-brown undercoat. Darker shading along the spine; tail tipped with black, and without rings. Black between the toes, with colour extending up the back of

Below: A Sorrel (Red) Abyssinian. An elegant, colourful pet. More responsive and doglike than most.

the hind legs. Tips and edges of ears black or dark brown. Noseleather brick red. Paw pads black. Eyes green, yellow or hazel rimmed with black or dark brown, encircled by a paler area. 118 ▶

Sorrel (Red). Body colour a rich copper red, ticked with dark red or chocolate brown, with paler apricot undercoat. Darker spine and tail tip. Chocolate colour between the toes extends up the back of the hind legs. Noseleather and paw pads pink. Tips and edges of ears chocolate brown. White allowed only on lips and chin. Eyes green, yellow or hazel, the more brilliant and deep the colour the better. Pale eyes are a fault. 118 ▶

Blue. Body colour a soft warm blue-grey, ticked with a darker steel blue. Base hair is cream or oatmeal. Spine, tail tip and back of hind legs dark steel blue. Tips and edges of ears slate blue. Noseleather dark pink. Paw pads mauve-blue. Eyes green, yellow or hazel. Pale eyes are considered a fault.

146

SINGAPURA

Good points
- *Pretty*
- *Responsive*
- *Relatively quiet*
- *Loves people*
- *Can be trusted with babies*
- *Easy to groom*
- *Lively*

Take heed
- *No drawbacks known*

The Singapura is known as the 'drain cat' of Singapore. In its native country, a large section of the community regards cats with suspicion, and consequently the native cats have to fend for themselves and are reserved and suspicious by nature. Foreigners living in the area have befriended some of them, and once they know no harm is intended, they become less shy and more trusting and responsive.

Several of these cats have been taken to the United States and are now becoming established as a new breed. With human care, the Singapura is an affectionate cat, though quiet and a little demure. It is generally smaller than other domestic cats, possibly because of its deprived ancestry.

In Singapore the cats are of many different colours and patterns, but those imported into the United States have ticked ivory and brown coats and golden eyes.

The breed is now receiving much publicity and there is a waiting list for kittens, both as pets and for breeding. As would be expected, Singapuras love to eat ocean fish!

Grooming
A Singapura needs very little grooming: just the normal daily comb through and, from time to time, attention to the ears and eyes.

Origin and history
The Singapura is a natural breed from Southeast Asia, where the majority of the native cats have ticked coats resembling those of

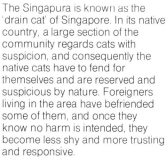

Abyssinians, but are smaller and have different features. Generally roaming free and taking shelter in the drains of Singapore, these cats have been adopted by foreigners living on the island and have been given a standard for competition both in Singapore and in the United States. They were first shown in the United States in 1977, but are still extremely rare.

Breeding
As with many natural breeds, the queens make excellent and sensible mothers. Normally there are only three kittens in the litter, and unlike most Oriental-type Shorthairs, which are usually very precocious, both male and female may not mate for the first time until they are 15 to 18 months old.

Kittens
Singapura kittens mature slowly and often do not come out of the nesting box until five weeks old.

SHOW SUMMARY
The Singapura is a very small cat, but alert and healthy with noticeably large, cupped ears and large eyes.
Coat. Very fine, short, silky and close-lying. A little longer in kittens.
Body. Smaller than average: females 1.8kg (4lb) or less; males 2.7kg (6lb) or less. Medium long body, moderately stocky, dense and muscular. Back slightly arched, medium long legs and small tight paws. Body, legs and floor should form a square. Neck short and thick with high shoulder blades.

Tail. Medium long, tapering to a blunt tip. No kinks.

Head. Rounded, narrowing to a blunt, medium short muzzle with a definite whisker break. Full chin. In profile a slight break well down the bridge of the nose. Ears large, slightly pointed, wide open at the base and possessing a deep cup. Small ears are a show fault.

Eyes. Large, almond-shaped, wide open and slanted.

Colour. Each hair on the back and flanks and top of the head must have at least two bands of dark brown ticking separated by bands of lighter, warm, old-ivory ticking. The tip of each hair should be dark and the base light. A darker line along the spine is permitted, ending in a dark tail tip. Legs without barring preferred. Toes dark brown, the colour extending up the back of the hind legs. Muzzle, chin, chest and stomach should be a warm pale fawn. Ruddier tones are allowed on the ears and the bridge of the nose. White lockets or white hairs are faults. Eyes, nose and lips are rimmed in dark brown. Nose-leather red, paw pads dark brown. Eyes hazel, green or gold. 118 ▶

Below: One of the new colours to appear in Singapuras, a combination of ticked tabby and white markings.

REX

Good points
- *Hardy and agile*
- *Great sense of fun*
- *Loves people*
- *Takes readily to cars or to a harness and lead*
- *Very easy to groom*

Take heed
- *Has a voracious appetite, but overfeeding will cause obesity*

Cornish Rex   Devon Rex

Despite its short coat, the Rex does not appear to feel the cold. It does not need coddling and is quite hardy in even the coldest weather. It is a pretty, unusual-looking cat with a coat of curly hair and curly whiskers and eyebrows. Characteristically, the coat feels warm to the touch because the hair is so fine and short.

There are two types of Rex — the Cornish and the Devon — and although similar in many ways, the Devon Rex is particularly playful, and its pixie-like face betrays a devilish sense of mischief. It is also said to wag its tail like a dog when

Below: A charming and playful pair of white Devon Rex kittens. Note the exceptionally big ears, which are a feature of the breed.

pleased. Intelligent and enterprising, both Rexes make excellent pets for all the family.

One point to watch, however; the Rex has a tendency to over-eat and can easily ruin its streamlined figure. Overfeeding should be avoided as a fat Rex is particularly unattractive.

Grooming
Rexes are very easy to groom. All that is needed is a silk cloth or a chamois leather to polish the coat, and lots of hand grooming to remove any dead hairs. Before a show it is a good idea to give a bran bath to remove any grease in the coat, which might upset the flow of the waves and curls. If the coat is really dirty and requires a wet bath, it is advisable to do this a

couple of weeks before a show, as the curl goes limp immediately after a bath.

Origin and history

The two strains of these curly-coated cats appeared as natural mutations in England, the United States, Germany and Canada almost simultaneously. The Cornish Rex is so called because it first appeared in Bodmin, Cornwall, in 1950, in an otherwise normal litter of farm cats. It was named after the Rex rabbit, which also has a curly coat. The curly kitten was mated back to its mother, and this produced more curly-coated kittens. Some of the offspring were imported into the United States, as were some from Germany. These, when mated together, appeared to be compatible, as they produced all curly-coated kittens. However, another strain of curly-coated cats appeared in a litter of kittens in Devon, England, in 1960, and these, when mated to the Cornish Rex, were obviously incompatible, as they produced all straight-coated kittens. Hence two separate varieties of Rex cat are recognized and should not be intermated, as they are genetically quite different.

The Rex was first recognized as a breed in 1967 and is now accepted in all countries of the world. Rex cats from England have been imported into Australia and New Zealand, and New Zealand breeders have introduced the Rex gene into Manx stock. Theoretically, it is possible to rex the coat of any breed of cat, but a longhaired Rex is not being bred, as the coat tends to be lank and unattractive. The first all Rex cat show was held in Kentucky, November 1980.

Breeding

Mating two Cornish Rexes together and two Devon Rexes together produces 100 percent Rex-coated kittens. By mating a Rex to a Siamese, the Himalayan coat pattern is introduced and the very attractive Si-Rex is obtained. Rex queens kitten easily and make good mothers.

Kittens

Rex kittens are robust and healthy. They will certainly keep you busy, being highly active, precocious and mischievous.

CORNISH REX

SHOW SUMMARY

Although the original curly-coated kittens were British Shorthair type (as they were produced from British farm stock), a more stream-lined 'Foreign' type is now preferred on the show bench; the cat should be fine-boned and elegant with a longer wedge-shaped face and a long whip tail.

Coat. Short, thin hair, but dense, plush and close-lying. No guard hairs. The hair should curl, wave or ripple, especially on the back and tail, but preferably all over, even on the paws. Whiskers and eyebrows should also be curly. Too short or

Below: A Cornish Si-Rex Lilac-point, an interesting combination of Himalayan coat pattern with curly coat type.

shaggy a coat or hairless patches
are faults.
Body. Hard, muscular, medium in
size but slender, not cobby,
standing high on long, straight
legs. Back arched. Paws small,
dainty and oval.
Tail. Long, thin and tapering.
Head. Modified Foreign type with
medium length wedge, flat skull
and straight profile with no nose
break. Ears large, set high on the
head, wide at the base, rounded at
the tips, covered in fine short fur.
Eyes. Oval and medium in size. 119 ▶

DEVON REX

SHOW SUMMARY
The Devon Rex has a coarser coat
than the Cornish Rex, but is similar
in build, being muscular yet dainty,
but different in face. A firm,
medium-sized cat with a long tail
and huge ears.
Coat. Very short, fine, wavy and
soft, not shaggy, but coarser than
that of the Cornish, due to the
presence of minute guard hairs.
Short curly whiskers and
eyebrows, which tend to be brittle.
Body. Medium in size, slender,
hard and muscular. Broad in the
chest; carried high on long, slim
legs. Hind legs generally longer
than forelegs. Feet small and oval.
Tail. Long, fine and tapering,
covered with short curly fur. No
kinks.

*Above: A Dilute Calico (US)
Cornish Rex. The breed is only
about thirty years old but it already
has many devotees, worldwide.*

Head. A rounded wedge with a flat
top, set on a slender neck.
Rounded cheeks with a whisker
break, and a definite nose break in
profile. Ears set low on the head,
very large, with or without ear
muffs and tufts; wide at the base,
rounded at the tips, and covered in
very fine soft fur.
Eyes. Wide-set, large, oval and
slightly slanted.

REX COLOURS
Most colours and coat patterns are
acceptable for competition,
including the Himalayan coat
pattern (Si-Rex). In the United
Kingdom in the Cornish Rex any
white markings should be symmetrical (except in Tortoiseshell-
and-white), and in the Devon Rex
any white markings are unaccept-
able (except in Tortoiseshell-and-
white), as are Bicolours at present.

In the United States chocolate,
lilac and Si-Rex are not acceptable at the present time, but most
other colours and combinations of
colours and patterns are currently
recognized.

Eye colour should be in keeping
with the coat colour or pale green,
yellow or gold. White Rex may be
gold-, blue- or odd-eyed (one gold,
one blue); Si-Rex must be blue. 119 ▶

AMERICAN WIREHAIR

Good points
- *Interestingly different*
- *Sturdy and robust*
- *Sweet tempered*
- *Affectionate*
- *Adaptable*
- *Agile*
- *Intelligent*

Take heed
- *No drawbacks known*

The American Wirehair is an American shorthaired or domestic cat with a distinctive wiry coat that is hard and springy to the touch, and not unlike sheep's wool in texture. It is bred in all colours and is an interestingly different kind of cat to have as a pet. Not prone to illness, the Wirehair is a sturdy breed.

It will take a lively interest in its surroundings and is intelligent, active and agile. Being very sweet natured and affectionate, it makes an ideal family pet. However, as it is one of the more recent breeds on the cat scene it is relatively rare.

Grooming
Virtually no grooming is necessary. A gentle brushing with a soft brush once or twice a week will remove loose hairs. Plenty of hand stroking will help to keep the coat in good condition. It is essential to shampoo. This can be done just before a show; the hair springs quickly back into place.

Origin and history
The American Wirehair is a natural mutation that occurred in an otherwise normal Domestic Shorthair litter. Each of the hairs is hooked at the end and wavy along its length. The first to be recorded was at Verona, New York, in 1966, although it has also been recorded that kittens with identical coats were seen on London bomb sites after the Second World War. This strain now seems to have died out and may therefore have been sterile. Kittens from the American matings have now been exported to Canada and Germany.

Breeding
Wirehairs mated to normal-coated shorthaired cats will produce 50 percent wirehaired kittens. The gene is not linked to colour and all coat patterns are possible.

Kittens
Wirehair kittens are born with tight curly coats. They are healthy, playful and robust. An average litter contains four or five kittens.

SHOW SUMMARY
The overall impression of the American Wirehair is of a medium-sized cat, rounded and woolly rather like a lamb.
Coat. The distinctive feature of this cat is its unique coat, which is of medium length and tightly curled. Body type is American Shorthair. All the hairs are crimped, even in the ears, and hooked at their ends. In some places, particularly on the head, the hair forms into ringlets rather than waves. The whiskers are crimped or wavy and untidy.

The unique coat is formed by a change in the structure of the guard hairs (those of the top coat), which are normally smooth and tapering but have become crimped along the shaft, hooked at their ends and thinner than normal guard hairs. This gives rise to a woolly coat, which is thick, coarse, resilient and springy to the touch. The hair on the chin, chest and stomach is slightly less coarse.
Body. Medium to large, well-muscled, with shoulders the same width as haunches. Back level. Legs medium long; paws oval and compact.

Tail. Moderately full, tapering to a rounded tip.

Head. Round, with prominent cheekbones, well-developed muzzle and chin and a slight whisker break. Face bright and alert: medium long, thick muscular neck. Nose is concave in profile. Ears medium in size, set wide apart with rounded tips.

Eyes. Large, round, bright and clear, set well apart, at an angle.

Below: A Silver Tabby American Wirehair. The hard, springy fur appeared as a natural mutation. Distinctive and robust, this breed is still something of a rarity in the international cat world.

AMERICAN WIREHAIR COLOURS

All colours and coat patterns are permissible and possible, and include solid white, black, blue, red and cream; chinchilla, shaded silver, shell cameo, cameo tabby, shaded cameo, black smoke, blue smoke, cameo smoke; tortoise-shell, calico, dilute calico, blue-cream; bicolour; classic and mackerel tabby patterns in silver, brown, red, blue and cream; and any other colour or pattern, or combination of colours and patterns with white, with the exception of the Himalayan pattern or chocolate and lilac (lavender). Eye colour appropriate to coat. 120 ▶

SPHYNX (Moon Cat; Canadian Hairless)

Good points
- *Hardy, not susceptible to cold*
- *Needs no brushing or combing*
- *Certainly attracts attention*
- *Affectionate*
- *Loyal*
- *Quiet*
- *Good natured*

Take heed
- *Should be sponged regularly*

The hairless cat is an unusual animal and may not be to everyone's taste. The body feels hot and smooth to the touch, as there is little fur to act as a temperature barrier or to insulate the body warmth; however the Sphynx does not seem to feel the cold as might be expected.

Unlike other cats, the Sphynx sweats and leaves a dander on the skin which has to be sponged periodically.

It is an affectionate and good natured cat, quiet yet loyal. Its distinctive appearance certainly attracts attention at a show.

Grooming
No brushing or combing is required, but the dander that accumulates on the skin should be sponged away with warm water daily or as necessary.

Origin and history
Hairless kittens have appeared in litters of ordinary Domestic Shorthairs and other breeds in France, England (in connection with the Devon Rex) and Canada. It is the Canadians who, since 1966, have taken an interest in this breed and have developed a breeding programme to perpetuate it. This began in 1966 in Ontario, when a hairless male kitten was born to a Black-and-White Domestic Shorthair.

It is thought that the Aztecs had hairless cats, and some were recorded in Mexico at the end of the nineteenth century and known as Mexican Hairless. These are now thought to be extinct. Unlike

the Sphynx they grew fine winter hair that moulted in the summer.

Breeding
Hairless cats breed true to type, but can also be produced from normal-coated cats carrying the gene for hairlessness. Outcrosses to Domestic Shorthairs are used from time to time to improve stamina, and do not seem to affect the Sphynx body type.

Kittens
Sphynx kittens are born with a fine covering of soft, short hair most of which is lost as they approach adulthood, when any hair is confined to the face, paws, tail tip and testicles in males. Kittens are usually bow-legged at first and have wrinkled and rather loose skins that appear to be too big for them.

SHOW SUMMARY
The Sphynx is a medium-sized cat, fine-boned but powerful, without hair on most of its body.
Coat. There is a short velvet pile covering the face and ears, that is longest and heaviest on the nose and sides of the mouth. The paws are also covered with fine hair up to the ankles, as is the end of the tail. There is a ridge of fine hair on the back and the testicles are covered in long, close-lying hair. Too much hair is a fault.
Body. Long, fine-boned and muscular. The skin is taut without wrinkles, except on the head. The legs are long and slim with small round paws; hind legs are slightly longer than forelegs.

Tail. Long, thin and hard. No kinks.
Head. Neither round nor wedge-shaped; flat between the eyes. The neck is fairly long and the chin square. The short nose is covered with velvet-like fur and there is a decided nose break. The ears are very large, wide at the base and rounded at the tips, sticking out from the head at the lobes.
Eyes. Deep set and slanted.

SPHYNX COLOURS

All colours and coat patterns are allowed (see American Wirehair), excluding the Himalayan pattern, chocolate, lilac (lavender), or any of these with white.

A pink locket at the neck is acceptable but white is allowed only around the nipples and navel. Particoloured patterns should be arranged symmetrically. Eyes gold, green or hazel, or in keeping with the coat colour. 120 ▶

Below: The Sphynx is a most unusual looking cat but has its devotees, no doubt because of its quiet, affectionate nature.

Further Reading

Alcock, James *A Cat of Your Own*
  Sheldon Press, London 1980
Ashford & Pond *Rex, Abyssinian & Turkish*
  John Gifford Ltd, London 1972
Beadle, Muriel *The Cat History, Biology & Behaviour*
  William Collins, Sons & Co Ltd Glasgow
Burgess, Grace *Cats & Common Sense*
  Price Milburn, New Zealand 1973
Catac Publications *All About Shows & Showing*
  Catac Publications, Bedford, England 1979 (Reprint)
Dunhill, Mary *Siamese Cat Owners Encyclopaedia*
  Pelham Books Ltd, London 1978 (Reprint)
Epton, Nina *Cat Manners & Mysteries*
  Michael Joseph, London 1973
Faler, Kate *This is the Abyssinian Cat*
  TFH Publications Inc. N.J. USA 1981
Feline Advisory Bureau *Boarding Cattery Construction & Management*
  Feline Advisory Bureau 1979 (Reprint)
Fireman, Judy *Cat Catalog*
  Workman Publishing Co, New York, USA 1976
Greer, Milton *The Fabulous Feline*
  Dial Press, New York, USA 1961
Henderson & Coffey *Cats & Cat Care*
  David & Charles 1973
Joshua, Joan *Cat Owners Encyclopedia Veterinary Medicine*
  TFH Publications Inc, N.J. USA 1979
Jude, A.C. *Cat Genetics*
  TFH Publications Inc, N.J. USA 1977 (Reprint)
Kirk, Hamilton *The Cat's Medical Dictionary*
  Routledge & Kegan Paul 1956
Lauder, P. *The Siamese Cat*
  B.T. Batsford Ltd, London 1978 (reprint)
Linzey, Andrew *Animal Rights*
  SCM Press Ltd 1976
Lippman, M *Cat Training (How To Do Tricks!)*
  TFH Publications Inc, N.J. USA 1974
Loxton, Howard *Guide to the Cats of the World*
  Elsevier Phaidon, Oxford, England 1975
MacBeth & Booth *The Book of Cats*
  Secker & Warburg Ltd, London 1976
Manolson, Frank *C is for Cat*
  Pan Books Ltd, London 1979 (Reprint)
Manolson, Frank *My Cat's in Love*
  Pelham Books Ltd, London 1970
Manton, S.M. *Colourpoint, Longhair & Himalayan Cats*
  Ferendue Books 1979 (Reprint)
McCoy J.J. *Complete Book of Cat Health & Care*
  Herbert Jenkins Ltd, London 1969
McDonald Brearley, J. *All About Himalayan Cats*
  TFH Publications Inc, N.J. USA 1976
McGinnis, Terrie *The Well Cat Book*
  Wildwood House Ltd, London 1976
Meins & Floyd *Groom Your Cat*
  TFH Publications Inc, N.J. USA 1972
Mery, Fernand *The Life, History & Magic of the Cat*
  Paul Hamlyn, London 1967

Moyes, Penny *How To Talk To Your Cat*
   Arthur Barker Ltd, London 1979 (Reprint)
Naples, Marge *This Is The Siamese Cat*
   TFH Publications Inc, N.J. USA 1978 (Reprint)
Nelson Vera M. *Siamese Cat Book*
   TFH Publications Inc, N.J. USA 1976 (Reprint)
Pond, Grace *The Cat (The Breeds, the Care & the Training)*
   Orbis Publishing Ltd, London 1980 (Reprint)
Pond, Grace *Complete Cat Encyclopaedia*
   W H Heinemann, London 1979 (Repeat)
Pond, Grace *Observers Book of Cats*
   Frederick Warne (Publishers) Ltd 1979 (Reprint)
Pond, Grace *Pictorial Encyclopaedia of Cats*
   Purnell Books, Maidenhead, Berks, England 1980
Pond & Raleigh, G & I *Standard Guide to Cat Breeds*
   Macmillan London Ltd, London 1979
Pond & Sayer *Intelligent Cat*
   Davis-Poynter Ltd, London 1977
Ramsdale, J. *Persian Cats & Other Longhairs*
   TFH Publishing Inc, N.J. USA 1976 (Reprint)
Robinson, Roy *Genetics For Cat Breeders*
   Pergamon Press Ltd, Oxford, England 1978 (Reprint)
Sayer, Angela *Encyclopaedia of the Cat*
   Octopus Books Ltd, London 1979
Sheppard, K *The Treatment of Cats by Homoeopathy*
   Health Science Press, Holsworthy, Devon 1960
Silkstone Richards, Pocock, Swift & Watson *The Burmese Cat*
   B.T. Batsford Ltd, London 1979 (Reprint)
Silkstone Richards, D. *Pedigree Cat Breeding*
   B.T. Batsford Ltd, London 1977
Smythe, R.H. *Cat Psychology*
   TFH Publications Inc, N.J. USA
Soderberg, P.M. *A.B.C. Cat Diseases*
   TFH Publications Inc, N.J. USA 1967
Thies, Dagmar *Cat Breeding*
   TFH Publications Inc, N.J. USA 1980 (Reprint)
Thies, Dagmar *Cat Care*
   TFH Publications Inc, N.J. USA 1980 (Reprint)
T.V. Vet *Cats Their Health & Care*
   Farming Press Ltd, Suffolk, England 1977
Urcia, Ingeborg *All About Rex Cats*
   TFH Publications Inc, N.J. USA 1981
Urcia, Ingeborg *This is the Russian Blue*
   TFH Publications Inc, N.J. USA 1981
West, Geoffrey *All About Your Cat's Health*
   Pelham Books Ltd, London 1980
Williams, Kathleen *Siamese Cats* (Foyles Handbook)
   W & G Foyle Ltd, London 1980 (Reprint)
Wilson, Meredith D *Encyclopedia of American Cat Breeds*
   TFH Publications Inc, N.J. USA 1978
Wolfgang, Harriet *Short Haired Cats*
   TFH Publications Inc, N.J. USA 1963
Wright & Walters, M & S *The Book of the Cat*
   Pan Books Ltd, London 1980
Zimmerman, Ruth *Abyssinians*
   TFH Publications Inc, N.J. USA 1980

Index

The main text articles on each breed are indexed in Roman type. Other entries in the index refer only to illustrations: *italic* type for photographs and **bold** type for colour artwork.

Index

Above: A Turkish Cat, white with auburn markings.

Credits

Colour and line artwork
John Francis (Linden Artists)
©Salamander Books Ltd.

Photographs
The publishers wish to thank the
following photographers and
agencies who have supplied
photographs for this book.

Alice Su: 45, 47, 54, 67, 71, 74,
85, 90, 91, 95, 103, 108, 116,
120, 130, 151, 155

Animals Unlimited (Paddy Cutts):
133, 137

Creszentia: 33, 59, 88, 107, 153

Anne Cumbers: 105

Marc Henrie: 8, 11, 12, 13, 14, 17,
18, 21, 22, 24, 27, 29, 31, 34, 37,
38, 40, 42, 49, 50, 51, 52, 53, 55,
56, 57, 58, 60, 61, 62, 63, 64, 65,
69, 72, 76, 78, 79, 81, 83, 93, 97,
98, 99, 100, 101, 106, 109, 110,
111, 112, 113, 114, 115, 117, 118,
119, 121, 123, 124, 127, 129,
132, 134, 135, 141, 142, 145,
146, 148, 149, 150. Half-title,
title page and endpapers.

Jane Howard: 87

Jayne Langdon: 138

Editorial assistance
Copy-editing and proof-reading:
Maureen Cartwright.
Index: Bridget Gibbs.

PRINTED IN BELGIUM BY
INTERNATIONAL BOOK PRODUCTION

Ruddy Somali kitten